Praise for *E*

"Very compelling and personal... fragrant details, great zoom-lens scenes of Palestinian family life... pull us right into the landscape and the domain... I support this book and salute its honesty and stirring intentions. We need it in our world. We need every single politician to have a copy in his/her back pocket. As the daughter of a Palestinian also from Jerusalem, I can say that this book rings deeply true to me, and assuages my sorrow somewhat over all the injustice which has pervaded the Holy City for far too long... Nammar makes a strong stride in all the right directions."
—Naomi Shihab Nye, award-winning author, writer, and poet

"I cannot think of a more appropriate reading on the Nakba—the catastrophe of displacement of most of the native Palestinians—than this searing and honest story of the family of Jacob Nammar. This poignant story of one Jerusalemite family provides a microcosm for the stories of hundreds of thousands of Palestinian Christian and Muslim families. Nammar's narrative is never bitter and instead provides a message of perseverance against all odds, a message of hope for peace and justice, and a message to remind us of our common humanity. Told with exquisite detail and beauty... this readable memoir will help many people around the world understand the reality of Palestine and its dispossessed people."
—Mazin B. Qumsiyeh, author of *Sharing the Land of Canaan*

"This is a compelling and compassionate memoir of a Jerusalem life during wartime and after... stands out as one of very few works that addresses the life for those Palestinians who stayed behind in the Israeli occupied part of (West) Jerusalem... On this level the book is original and has significant ethnographic value for the historical researcher, as well as for students of the Arab-Israeli conflict."
—Salim Tamari, editor, *Jerusalem Quarterly,*
Institute of Jerusalem Studies

"This not just the story of a single, large extended Palestinian family living before and after the Nakba in 1948. The Nammar family is at the center of a large tapestry in which Palestinian history, cultural roots, and traditions are carefully woven. The description of al-Quds, where the family lived, moves deeply..."
—Mohammed Omer, photojournalist

BORN IN JERUSALEM, BORN PALESTINIAN
A MEMOIR

JACOB J. NAMMAR
FOREWORD BY SALIM TAMARI

*To Adam,
For Peace, Love
Nammar*

OLIVE
BRANCH
PRESS

An imprint of Interlink Publishing Group, Inc.
www.interlinkbooks.com

First published in 2012 by

OLIVE BRANCH PRESS
An imprint of Interlink Publishing Group, Inc.
46 Crosby Street, Northampton, Massachusetts 01060
www.interlinkbooks.com

Library of Congress Cataloging-in-Publication Data
Nammar, Jacob J., 1941–
 Born in Jerusalem, born Palestinian : a memoir / by Jacob J. Nammar.
    p. cm. Includes bibliographical references.
 ISBN 978-1-56656-886-9 (pbk.)
 1. Nammar, Jacob J., 1941–2. Palestinian Arabs—Jerusalem—Biography.
 3. Businessmen—Texas—San Antonio—Biography. 4. Jerusalem—
 History—Partition, 1948. I. Title.   DS109.93.N36 2012
 956.94'4204092--dc23   [B]   2012007636

Printed and bound in the United States of America

To request our complete 48-page full-color catalog, please call us toll free
at 1-800-238-LINK, visit our website at www.interlinkbooks.com, or
write to Interlink Publishing, 46 Crosby Street, Northampton, MA 01060
e-mail: info@interlinkbooks.com

CONTENTS

ACKNOWLEDGMENTS

I thank Salim Tamari for encouraging my work on this memoir and writing the foreword, Mazin Qumsiyeh and Lana Ulrich for their exceptional guidance and advice, and my faithful friend Naomi Shihab Nye for her steadfast belief and support. My utmost gratitude goes to my dearest lifetime friend Clarence Thomson for his inspiration and assistance, to my wife Lesley for her patience and devotion, to my brothers and sisters for sharing their stories and reminding me of our childhood in Jerusalem, to my daughters Jacquetta and Jeneen, and my son Joseph. I am deeply grateful to the Interlink team: Michel Moushabeck, publisher; John Fiscella, editing; Leyla Moushabeck, book design and layout; Julian Ramirez, map design; Pam Fontes-May, cover design; and Sara Rauch, proofreading.

I dedicate this memoir to my father Yousef, to my mother Tuma, and to the countless Palestinian men, women, and children whose lives were lost in the struggle for justice, freedom, and peace.

FOREWORD

Jacob Nammar has the unique distinction of being a member of the only family in Jerusalem after whom a neighborhood is named. Nammareh (or al-Nammareh), in Lower Baq'a, was a pioneering community that evolved outside the city walls in the nineteenth century, when enhanced municipal security and gas lighting allowed members of the mercantile families to escape the crowding of the Old City. The Nammaris joined the Khalilis, the Jarallahs, the Husseinis, and several other propertied clans to venture into the middle-class mansions in the new suburbs of Bab al-Sahira, Musrara, Sheikh Jarrah, and Baq'a. In mid-century these were isolated communities facing the walls of the city and the olive orchards, which surrounded their abodes. Within decades they were joined by the new Jewish communities of Montefiore and Me'a She'arim, and the Greek Orthodox suburbs of Qatamon and Talbieh. Thus the New City was born.

But Jacob Nammar's autobiographic narrative is compelling for a different reason. In the war of 1948 virtually every Palestinian Arab who lived in the villages and townships to the west of the city, around 200,000 people, were expelled to the East beyond the Armistice lines. A much smaller Jewish community from the Old City was also displaced and relocated to the West. The Nammari family, whose gripping story is told here, is one of the very few who managed to remain in the area that was taken over by Haganah and other Jewish paramilitary forces. Unlike the situation in the Galilee, in the Triangle, and in Negev, where the remaining Arab minority managed to stay put and grew up to constitute the Arab minority in Israel—the Nammaris and the handful of Arabs that found themselves in West Jerusalem in the spring of 1948, were an anomaly. They survived by virtue of a mistake of military logistics and had to fend for themselves after the total collapse of their society, and the mass expulsion of their compatriots.

Nammar's story has not been heard before, because virtually nobody was left to tell it. Virtually, because we do have the important chronicle of John Rose, *The Armenians of Jerusalem*, which tells the story of an Armenian family left for several years in Talbieh, before Rose and his family were relocated to the eastern part of the city in the mid-fifties.[1] Like John, Jacob also had an Armenian mother, whose origins from Yerevan and torturous journey to Palestine are captured in these memoirs in the context of the Armenian genocide. Is it an accident that the two surviving narratives of Palestinians who remained in West Jerusalem had an Armenian connection?

In both Nammar's and John Rose's account of the war, the year 1949 seems to have been a crucial year. It was the year when the nascent Israeli state began to consolidate its hold on Arab "abandoned" property and to deal with those

Palestinians who remained inside the territories of the Jewish state. In Jerusalem the occupied city was divided into three zones, A, B, and C—similar (but not equivalent) to the divisions of the western city established by the British during WWII. The dozen or so families who, like the Nammaris, found themselves hostages to the new situation, were forced to relocate to each of these zones in order to monitor and control their movements. Most often their new habitat was not located in their original home area, which they were compelled to abandon for "security reasons." The explanation used for this internal displacement was that the remaining residents were absentees, and their homes were sequestered even though the families in question were in fact still in situ. They became absentees in their own homeland, together with tens of thousands of other "absentees" from the Galilee and the Triangle regions. Jiryis al-Salti was another compatriot of Jacob Nammar who, like him, was forced to relocate from Baq'a. He also left a unique diary of his experience, which illuminates, replicates, and confirms the two accounts of Rose and Nammar. Here is al-Salti, recounting the days of the creation of the 1949 ghetto and its consequence, as told by historian Issam Nassar:

> ... The creation of the zone was not good news for the few who lived outside it. They were told that for their own protection they had to move into an abandoned house of their choice within the fenced area ... The Saltis were among those whose houses were outside of the zone and were therefore, forced to move into somebody else's house inside the zone. Arab homes outside the zone were given by the authorities to Jews who needed homes with the aim of creating a new reality on the ground that would prevent the possibility of having to turn them over to the Arab side. But as the houses outside of the zone became occupied, Jews were now coming into the zone

and taking over empty homes there. In fact, as Salti's journal illustrated, Jews were starting to take over even inhabited Arab houses in the zone as well taking over sections and rooms in those houses. On October 19, 1949, Salti wrote, "the situation is getting worst. The Jews are squatting even in inhabited Arab houses aiming to take over a room." Eager to take over Arab homes, some Israeli zealots from outside of the area would drive noisy motorcycles in *al-Baq'a* in the late hours of the night making a commotion and hoping to scare off residents forcing them to leave the area and to abandon their homes.[2]

By the end of 1949 the military zones were abolished in Jerusalem, but through the Military Government the Israeli administration continued to regulate the lives of the remaining Palestinians in the country until 1966, some two decades later. It is quite intriguing, and an indication of the total isolation of the remaining Palestinian community in Jerusalem, that neither the Nammaris nor the Saltis were aware of each other's presence, even though they were literally living in adjacent compounds of the new ghetto.

For the historian of the Arab-Israeli conflict, the parts of this memoir that cover Nammar's life in Jerusalem after 1948 may hold special value. They deal with the family's expulsion from Baq'a and their removal to a confined area of the abandoned city, where they became a minority within a minority. Deserted by his neighbors, and finally by family, he had to fend for himself in a very hostile environment. He became the "enemy within," not through any fault of his own, but because his nation was defeated. Unlike the Palestinians who became a beleaguered minority in the northern districts, Nammar did not even have the benefit of being a member of a minority. In Jerusalem the family was dispersed again, by arrests, escapes, the death of the father, and the migration of his mother, sisters, and brothers, until Jacob remained alone.

His schooling at Terra Sancta, his sports career, his itinerant working career, and his daily encounters with the xenophobia of the Israeli state and its police apparatus are vignettes of internal exile in his own homeland, told with sardonic vividness, but also with a great deal of humor.

Engulfed by a Jewish society that saw him as an alien in his own country, he found his solace in the daily humdrum of survival. Throughout this tumultuous journey, Nammar lost neither hope nor faith in his fellow humans. His private personal predicament was absorbed in the national tragedy of his community. But he never abandons the sliver of hope in the redemption of his defeated nation. He maintains this hope in the kindness of strangers, and in the world of sports—in training a new generation of players, and in competing with his adversaries. He battled in an arena that he thought, mistakenly, would be free of national prejudice. He also maintains his faith by bonding with the transformed (and often unrecognizable) landscape of the familiar neighborhoods of his youth, and in the food of his childhood, in the land of *Zeit u Za'atar* as he calls it. Jacob's life is a narrative of hope, despair, and redemption through the love of a vanquished city.

Salim Tamari
Institute of Jerusalem Studies

[1] John H. Melkon Rose, *Armenians of Jerusalem: Memoirs of Life in Palestine* (London: Radcliffe Press, 1993).
[2] Issam Nassar, "A Liminal Existence in Jerusalem: al-Baq'a 1949," *Jerusalem Quarterly* 36 (Winter 2009).

"Take a stone from our house
So that our descendants
Will remember their way home."
—Mahmoud Darwish

1

THE HOUSE OF NAMMAR

I was born on May 16, 1941, in Madinat al-Quds, "the Holy City," known in the Western world as Jerusalem. I was born in the home of my father's parents in Haret al-Nammareh, the Nammareh neighborhood of Baq'a, or West Jerusalem.[1] Jerusalem has been inhabited for some ten thousand years, beginning in 4000 BC with the Canaanites, from whom the city's name originates. The name "Jerusalem" is derived from its Canaanitic root, Ur Salem, the House of Salem, a pagan god of the Canaanite clan known as the Jebusites.[2]

My birth certificate was issued by the Government of Palestine's Department of Health. It reads, "The above is true extract from the Register of Births kept at the Office of the Department of Health in the town of Jerusalem, with permanent address of parents in the District of Jerusalem Palestine," and is printed in English, Arabic, and Hebrew. Each of my brothers and sisters has an identical birth certificate. I have always treasured my birth certificate and saved it because the document confirms my birthright to al-Quds.

The city is composed of symbols that date back thousands of years. Ironically, Jerusalem is often referred to as the "City of Peace" despite its turbulent history of conflicts, wars, foreign imperial dominations, and tensions among competing religions. For the last three thousand years, it epitomized the heart and engine of Palestine. Prophets, scientists, scholars, artisans, merchants, and poets developed it to become the religious, cultural, and political center, not just of our part of the world but of civilization.

It is a unique place in the world and a holy city for the three Abrahamic religions of Judaism, Christianity, and Islam. It is, however, best known as the city of miracles—the location of Christ's resurrection, Mohammad's ascension to heaven, and Abraham's near sacrifice.

Jerusalem shaped my spirit, religion, heritage, identity, and earthly consciousness. There I always sensed the presence of God with me. My brothers, sisters, and I were baptized and confirmed in the Roman Catholic faith. Indigenous Palestinian Christians are descendants of those who first believed in Jesus Christ. We are families who have lived and worshipped in the land that gave birth to Christ and Christianity and where Jesus died and was resurrected. Palestinian Christians are a diverse group of almost all denominations: Catholic, Orthodox, Protestant, Anglican, and others. Christians have provided an important balance between Muslims and Jews in the Holy Land—a balance that existed since these three monotheistic religions came to share this region.

We were taught by our parents and the nuns and priests in our school that we were all God's children and spiritual descendants of Abraham, who introduced the one true God and was the father of these three religions indigenous to the Middle East. We believed in the biblical promise of the land to Abraham and his descendants. For centuries the natives of all three religions lived in harmony side by side.

My mother had many friends in the Armenian, Muslim, Jewish, and Christian Quarters of the Old City. She enjoyed many hours of socializing with friends, family, and neighbors. Mama made her rounds to the homes of her *Yahood* (Jewish) friends on Friday evenings, the Sabbath, to turn off their electric light switches for them, returning on Saturday nights to flip the switches back on. It was against the Jewish religion to work on the Sabbath, and turning the switches on and off was considered work.

One of my cousins, Zuheir al-Nammari, remembers how our family and the Jews in Jerusalem often helped each other. A few years ago, an Orthodox Jew showed him an old document. In the nineteenth century, the Jewish community needed to renovate their synagogue, as it was a huge building and very old. My family contributed two hundred gold Ottoman coins to the Jewish synagogue. The Orthodox Jew told my cousin, "Look, your family gave us that much to renovate. That was our relationship."[3]

We were a family of ten—my father, Yousef Rashid, my mother, Tuma Marie, one half-brother, three brothers, and three sisters. We were all healthy, energetic, and (we were told) good-looking. Mihran was the oldest, followed by Fahima, Daoud, Suleiman, Wedad, Fadwa, myself (Ya'coub), and Zakaria, with each child two years apart. Following the tradition in the Holy Land, my parents chose biblical names for the boys, after prophets of old, and expressive, descriptive names for the girls. My oldest sister Fahima's name in Arabic means "understanding," Wedad means "joy," and Fadwa means "patriotic." We were close and emotionally attached to each other. My parents hoped that their children would live up to their names by example, with faith and determination.

Everyone in my family had black hair and dark-colored eyes, as do most Palestinians. My eyes are the exception; they are *a'sali*, a honey-hazel color, that sometimes turns green in bright sunlight. Some other Palestinians in villages around al-Quds have green or blue eyes, and a few have blond hair. Stories say that these individuals may have mixed ancestry, with bloodlines dating back to the European Crusaders.

Nammar is our family's original name. The Nammar extended family, known also as *Nammari, al-Nammari,* or *Nammamreh* (plural), is a large family with relatives scattered throughout the world. They live in many countries, including Jordan, Saudi Arabia, Lebanon, Egypt, Iraq, Indonesia, Europe, North America, South America, and of course Palestine.

For many centuries the Nammamreh of Palestine were one of the leading families in al-Quds. It was believed that some members of our family who had their roots in al-Andalus of southern Spain were driven out in the eleventh century by King Ferdinand of Aragon and Queen Isabella of Castile, and settled and lived since then in the Holy City. The extended family members who remained in Palestine after the start of the Israeli occupation were tied to the land and each possessed a key to a home in Palestine.

My family owned several tracts of valuable properties in the Old City in Haret al-Nasara, the Christian Quarter, on al-Khanqa Street. This included several shops nearby in Suq al-A'ttarine, the spice market. In addition, they acquired land in 1870 from the villages of Malha and Beit Jala. In the late 1920s, the area had its own market, Suq al-Nammari, which served as a wholesale market for neighboring villages and a retail market for the local area. They owned several *bayarat*, or orchards, near Jaffa and a large house where once a year we vacationed and helped in the harvest of the citrus fruits. My family also owned a summer lake house in Tiberius, and some Nammamreh owned properties in the ancient city of Nablus, situated an hour's drive north of al-Quds, an area believed to be the biblical site of Jacob's well at the Greek Orthodox monastery.

In addition, in the villages of Yalu and Imwas the Nammamreh owned farms for the cultivation of grains, wheat, bulgur, and other produce. After each bountiful harvest, we received a large share of the yield to divide among all extended family members. My oldest sister Fahima remembers that each year the farmers came in a caravan of twelve camels, riding for seven days and seven nights. Highly regarded because they can retain large amounts of water and food for extended travel, and because they are faithful and obedient to their masters, the camels while in town were sheltered in our large yard. On one occasion, Fahima noticed one camel with beautiful long eyelashes crying in pain because he had a large nail stuck in one foot. It took four men to hold him down to pull the nail out and bind the wound to save him.

To secure their inheritance, the Nammamreh established various *waqfs*, endowment properties regulated by religious and secular laws, whose records were kept in the Old City court and administered by an elected family authority. These properties were nontransferable and forbidden to be sold for any religious, political, or historical claims. The aim was to keep the properties in the family for the benefit and needs of future generations. Each member of the family was entitled to receive revenues that they then passed on to their offspring.

In the mid-eighteenth century, al-Quds proper referred to what is now known as the "Old City." It was surrounded by a large, highly fortified wall with eight famous gates that were closed each night to protect the inhabitants. The city, one of the world's architectural marvels, was divided into four ethno-religious *haret*, or neighborhoods: Jewish, Muslim, Christian, and Armenian. As the Old City became over-crowded, several wealthy families ventured outside the wall, including some of the Nammamreh who branched out by developing a new suburb in the southwestern area of the city in the Lower Baq'a area. This was a bold undertaking since the land was barren, uninhabited, and filled with danger from robbers and wild animals.

However, the relocation from the Old City to the West New City created an exclusive community named Haret al-Nammareh or al-Nammariya—the Nammareh neighbor-hood. They built palatial homes with unique, spacious architectural designs including arched doorways, tile floors, high ceilings, and large windows for an upper-class lifestyle. These *qusur*, or villas, were built from carved limestone with large cream and pure-white stones that kept them warm in winter and cool in summer. The red tiled roofs, which shone beautifully at sunset on the hilltop, stood next to each other on both sides of a straight line which became known as the Share'a al-Nammareh—Nammareh Street.

The neighborhood originated from the efforts of the pioneer family of Abdullah Ibrahim Nammari, whose five boys and five girls built their own homes in the neighbor-hood. This tradition continued to evolve and grow over the years as cousins moved in, followed by other members of the extended family—including ours—which created a vibrant neighborhood. Ibrahim and many other family members were architects for centuries, specializing in art and drawing. In 1807 an Ottoman Sultanate decree was signed by Suleiman Pasha appointing a Nammari group as chief engineers for the city of Jerusalem. Because of this, the architecture of the city reflected a sophisticated and organized style as it developed rapidly. Our cousin Rafeeq al-Nammari was appointed *mukhtar,* the chief or elder, of Baq'a as the community grew larger.

———

My *Baba* (father), Yousef Rashid, was born in al-Quds in 1900. He wore Western clothes with a *tarbush* (red *fez)* Turkish hat, rather than a *keffiyeh,* the traditional Palestinian head-dress. He drove a tourist bus throughout the Middle East's major cities and was content with his job. He traveled to exotic cities such as Beirut, Amman, Damascus, Cairo, and major cities in Palestine. On one of his trips to Beirut he was introduced by a friend to a young woman from Armenia named Tuma. He began to court her and showered her and her son Mihran with gifts as is the traditional Palestinian custom. Ironically, Baba didn't speak Armenian, and Mama didn't speak Arabic. But fortunately they both could communicate in Turkish. He had become a frequent visitor to this beautiful Mediterranean city, and on each visit he became more attached and convinced she was to be his future wife.

My mother, Tuma, was born in Yerevan, Armenia, in 1910. When she was five, she witnessed her father, a judge, and the remainder of her family massacred by the Ottoman Turks. Between 1915 and 1918, the Ottoman Empire committed genocide against the Armenian population, and about 1,750,000 people, including women and children, were forcibly removed from their homeland and scattered around the world. A Turkish officer took Tuma to become a servant to his family in Diar Bakr, East Anatolia. One day, the officer's wife spilled boiling water on her arm, leaving her with a life-long scar. While in the hospital, Tuma was rescued by Armenian nuns belonging to an underground resistance group. They transported her to Beirut and placed her as an orphan at a Christian Catholic convent, where they taught her knitting and crochet. When she was fourteen the nuns arranged for Tuma to marry Ohannes Ovikian, a struggling young Armenian musician who died prematurely in a car accident, leaving her with a baby boy, named Mihran—my oldest stepbrother.

Shortly thereafter, Mama met a rich Italian couple who hired her to nurse their new baby because the mother was unable to feed him. Mama was capable and an excellent surrogate mother. For a year they traveled the Mediterranean on the man's yacht between Lebanon, Greece, and Italy. Unfortunately, after some time passed the man developed other designs for his baby nurse, so Mama left them and returned to the nuns in Beirut.

Unfortunately, the Nammamreh family did not approve of Baba's courtship, since they had other plans for him. He was to marry one of his cousins as was customary in his extended family. But Baba's mind was made up; he wanted Tuma. Thus on one of his last trips to Beirut he got married in an ecclesiastical court and adopted Mihran. As it was illegal at the time to cross from one country to the other, Baba daringly smuggled Mama and Mihran in the bus luggage compartment to al-Quds, against not only the authorities' regulations but also his own family's wishes. As a result, for a time Baba was disinherited and isolated from his extended family.

My father, Yousef Rashid Nammar (1946)

Baba was a classically tall, dark, and handsome man. He seemed like a large rock to me, powerfully built with authoritarian deep black eyes that could be stern but also gentle. He was peaceful and made us feel secure and valued and thus earned our complete respect. He was calm, understanding, did not raise his voice, and rarely used physical punishment.

To discipline us all he needed was to give a stern look. His penetrating glance would make us shiver. In contrast to Baba's strength, Mama was gentle, loving, and tender. She was beautiful, with fair skin and long silky hair. No wonder Baba fell in love with her, theirs was a romantic fairy tale full of passion and enduring love.

In the beginning, though, it was difficult for my mother to integrate with the Nammamreh family, especially the women and my father's sister, A'mmto (Aunt) Nafiseh. She was jealous, grouchy, and hard to live with. She never married and outlived every one of her generation.

Mama also wore Western clothes instead of a *thob*, the traditional Palestinian colorful embroidered dress. She devoted her life to raising her eight children and was constantly busy taking great care of us, keeping us healthy and safe during difficult times. Her home and family were her heart and soul. As a devout Armenian Christian, she always carried her little Bible with her. Early each morning she stood in front of the window and looked up toward heaven, raising her arms to pray in Armenian. I knew she was thinking of my Baba traveling because sometimes when I stood before that same window I would think of him, too.

My *sitto* (grandmother) loved Baba and was always kind to him. She became the driving force persuading the Nammamreh to gradually accept Baba's family. Baba and Mama then moved to the Haret al-Nammareh to live in his parent's spacious home.

2

OUR WAY OF LIFE

Shortly after moving into the home of my father's parents, Baba and Mama were blessed with the birth of my oldest sister Fahima, followed by six more beautiful children. We were all born at home in Haret al-Nammareh with the assistance of a midwife, which was customary as doctors were not readily available. Since we lived close to the German Colony, where the nuns ran an organized clinic and were helpful to us, Mama took us there regularly for checkups.

The only time I dreaded visiting the clinic was when I had a toothache and the nuns had to pull my tooth out with something like pliers, without novocain. I screamed throughout the process. Fortunately, we were all healthy and rarely saw doctors. But when we felt sick with headaches or stomach pains, Mama used traditional Palestinian homeopathic cures and had us drink hot boiled tea with either fresh mint or *babunej* (chamomile) leaves—wild green herbs found abundantly throughout the hills around the countryside.

Once in a while when we had a cold or muscle ache, Mama would bring out of the closet the famous antique *kasset al-hawa*, air cups. In this technique several round glass cups are placed a few inches apart on a patient's back after a small piece of paper is lit inside each cup. The cup creates a vacuum causing suction which draws out the pain after a few minutes when each cup is pulled off with a pop, leaving a red circular mark. Then the back is rubbed with olive oil to smooth and clean the skin.

My brothers, sisters, and I all believed in Mama. She inspired us, influenced our faith, and gave us a deep moral upbringing. She tried to keep a positive outlook, even in the face of the most difficult and trying moments, and in particular when her children made mistakes. One day I accidentally broke one of her favorite water glasses. I felt awful. Yet she did not scold me. All she said was, "You just broke the evil spell, don't be hard on yourself." Memories of my mother always remind me of one of my favorite philosophers, Kahlil Gibran, who said, "The mother is everything—she is our consolation in sorrow, our hope in misery, and our strength in weakness. She is the source of love, mercy, sympathy, and forgiveness."[4]

After all, Mama was our source of life, our first teacher, and a great storyteller, qualities that combined to help nurture us throughout childhood. At bedtime, she revealed to us how we were born and how proud she was. When Baba was gone, she would tell us stories, especially the exciting folktale adventures of *Alf Laylah Wa Laylah*—the stories of the *Thousand and One Nights*, perhaps the most famous of Arabian Nights classic literature. These fairy tales revolved around an evil king who swore vengeance against his adulterous wife and thereafter against all women. The king would marry and then soon command the death of his wife. Each

My mother, Tuma Marie Nammar (1946)

night he would marry a new young virgin and on the following morning put her to death. One evening the king chose a beautiful woman named Shahrazad. She was very clever and, as the legend portrays, a brilliant storyteller. Every night she would begin to tell the king a fascinating story but would end in the middle of the tale before the king fell asleep. Thus, the king would spare her so that he could hear the remainder of the story the following night. This continued night after night. Finally, after "a thousand and one nights" and after

Shahrazad had born the king three sons, he wised up, ceased his murderous tradition, and accepted her as his wife.

Mama's stories were fascinating, romantic, and exciting. She told tales of King Sinbad the Sailor, the Giant Genie, the Forty Thieves of Baghdad, Haroon Al Rashid, or the real-life Arab warrior Salah El Din (Saladin) who defeated the Crusaders from Europe. Sometimes they were humorous, spiced with tales of Juha, a popular Arab comic figure. But as we listened raptly all huddled together, or laughed together throughout the night, sometimes falling on top of one another, we wondered where Baba was. We knew that when he came home, we would all be together warm and safe.

I did not know much about Baba's journeys at the time. I knew he was gone, I didn't know where. I knew only that he was away and that it always seemed as if he had been gone forever. We were always eager to welcome him home, not because he brought us good news and gifts but because the family seemed restored when he returned. On occasions we kissed his hand to show him our respect and love.

We even often competed with each other to see who got to remove his shoes when he came home from work. One night while Baba was gone, I cuddled beside Mama as she told me a story. I was no more than five years old. When she finished, I whispered to her, "Mama, when Baba returns, I want to be the one who takes his shoes off." She kissed the top of my head. "Can I be the one who does that?" I implored. "Isn't it enough to kiss his hand?" she asked. "Please," I begged. "I want to take his shoes off." "Maybe," she said. "We'll see." What else could she say with eight children, all of whom would compete to take Baba's shoes off? But as I lay waiting for sleep, I did not think about Shahrazad. All I could think of was taking Baba's shoes off and wondering when he would be home.

A few weeks later I was playing fetch after school with our dog Laddie. We were playing tug of war with an olive branch stick. Suddenly Laddie let go and turned his attention to the street, wagging his tail and barking happily. I knew then that Baba was arriving home. We cheerfully ran to greet him. Mama welcomed him with open arms. She quickly remembered and whispered to Baba, "Ya'coub will be honored to take your shoes off and make you feel comfortable." Baba sat in his overstuffed chair next to the window over-looking the vegetable garden. I promptly bent down and removed his faded shoes and worn socks from his tired feet. I immediately noticed the bunions on his two big toes, which became a trademark in our family. I slipped my small feet into his large shoes, shuffling my way to his bedroom. Mama placed Baba's feet in a bucket of hot salted water to cleanse and relax them.

When I returned with Baba's slippers, I sat next to him. I could see in his eyes that my bringing the slippers was as meaningful to him as it was to me. We then gathered around Baba to hear about his trip to the beautiful city of Jaffa on the Mediterranean Sea.

Baba was eager to recount this particular trip even though the voyage had been hectic and exhausting. The bus was completely full of passengers, and it had been raining all day. As scheduled, he had made stops at several villages on his way to pick up and let off some passengers. At one of the stops, he saw a male passenger waving his hand in distress. Baba felt sorry for the desperate man waiting in the heavy rain, so he stopped to explain that the bus was full and did not have any seats available. Feeling sorry for him, Baba offered to let him ride on the roof of the bus with the baggage. Since there were no other accommodations, and the man was anxious to get to his destination, he agreed. On the roof among the baggage

My father Yousef (his bus in the background) with
a Palestinian armored border guard. (1945)

there was a wooden coffin being shipped to an unknown destination. As the rain started to come down heavier, the man decided to look inside the coffin. Finding it empty, he decided to climb in and lie in it for shelter from the rain.

At the next stop another man was anxiously waiting for a ride, even though none of the passengers were getting off the bus. Baba again felt sorry, so he invited the second man also to ride on top of the bus. As the bus continued on its journey to Jaffa, the man inside the coffin decided to check the condition of the rain. He opened the lid and extended his hand to feel the rain. The second man, seeing a hand coming out of the coffin, screamed with fear and jumped off the moving bus. The man in the coffin, hearing the commotion, also got scared and jumped out of the coffin and fell off the bus. With all the screaming and banging going on, Baba stopped the bus right away to investigate. To his astonishment, the two men were lying on the ground laughing hysterically, despite their bruises and aching limbs.

Sometimes, when Mama and Baba were busy, my sister Wedad, who loved to read, would tell us some of her favorite stories. One of them was about a traveling salesman who was handsome but not very smart. He wanted to marry a young, beautiful, and rich princess. However, the king did not approve and strongly objected to this "idiot," threatening to disinherit his daughter. But the princess decided to marry the salesman against her father's wishes to prove that she could make a smart man out of him. So she and her father placed a bet.

One day the salesman went on *hajj*, or pilgrimage, to the holy city of Mecca. En route he passed a well and heard a man crying for help. He stopped to assist. The man turned out to be a genie who gave the salesman a *rumannah* (pomegranate) in gratitude. He proceeded on his journey.

The salesman gave the *rumannah* to an acquaintance to deliver to his wife, along with a message of his love for her. Later that evening the princess decided to eat the *rumannah* while sitting on a stool in the garden. To her surprise she discovered that it was not a fruit but a container with valuable rubies inside. Being intelligent, she started to invest the rubies to build wealth for herself and her husband.

When the salesman returned from his voyage, his wife greeted him with love and affection and showed him to the new mansion she had built for them. In the meantime, the king asked, "Who has built this mansion in my kingdom?" He was told that it was his daughter, who had proven her ability to educate and make her husband wise and rich. So the daughter won the bet and lived happily ever after with her husband, as most fairy-tale princesses do.

I grew up at a time when these stories were both fond memories and fascinating tales because they taught me morality while helping me to fall asleep, all the while feeling enveloped in love. The stories were passed from one generation to the next and are cherished gems from my childhood. Moreover, I was influenced by the Arabic language, which is rich in proverbs for everything.

For example, Baba loved cars and owned an old antique, rusted Model T Ford. He regularly worked on this classic car while storing it in the corner of *Ammo* (Uncle) Rashid's carpentry workshop. Baba had a good sense of humor and periodically liked to tease and quiz me. He would ask me the answer to an old Arabic riddle: "*Esh tasa watarantasa fil bahar ghatasa juwata looloo wa barrata inhasa?*" ("What fruit is about the size of an apple, is full of rubies inside, is covered outside with copper-like skin, and sinks in the sea?") It's a *rumannah*—a pomegranate!

My parents grew up learning by experience, but they raised us to have both traditional wisdom passed down through stories, sayings, and prayers, along with a respect for formal schooling, something that neither of them ever had. It was a healthy combination. Over the years, my parents managed our large family well by teaching us love of God and of life, independent thinking, and the freedom to practice our religious beliefs. They emphasized the Ten Commandments and the traditional Palestinian value of respect for others, irrespective of their religion, race, or ethnicity. They taught us not to hate but to love everyone as children of God, and to believe in *karamah*—dignity and generosity. We were strictly forbidden—*haram*—to curse or use foul language; it was not in our vocabulary. We were raised spiritually—we learned religious tolerance and were reminded that "God will help those who help themselves."

Although he did not follow religious rituals, Baba believed in God and held deep and strong spiritual values. Yet, he did preserve the Palestinian Muslim tradition of circumcision for all of the boys. Mama was more religiously devoted; she enrolled all of us in Catholic schools. At our school I received my First Communion, and my certificate soberly proclaims, "*Ya'coub a fait sa premiere Communion dans l'Eglise du Pensionnal a Saint Joseph en 1948.*" Our parents placed great value on Christian upbringing and education. They enrolled us at French schools, which were the best private schools in the city. My sisters attended Saint Joseph Catholic School for Girls and my brothers and I attended the boys' Freres Jesuit Catholic School inside the Old City.

Al-Quds was a sacred place, understood and accepted worldwide as having provided freedom and equality for multireligious education. On top of this, we were a multilingual family. We all were taught several languages at home in addition to the basic educational curriculum we learned in school. Even though my mother's tongue was Armenian, we absorbed my father's language of Arabic. My father, in addition to Arabic, spoke Turkish and some English and Hebrew, while my mother spoke Armenian, Turkish, Arabic, Italian, and some Hebrew. My brothers and sisters spoke at least four languages; among them, Arabic, French, English, and some Armenian and Hebrew. This multilingual knowledge was extremely useful throughout our lives, not only for obvious reasons in aiding our educational and professional experiences but also for more lively communication among us. For example, my father and mother sometimes purposely spoke Turkish to each other so we could not understand what they were saying. We countered by speaking French among ourselves so that they, in turn, would be left in the dark. We were curious to hear them speak Turkish, especially late in the evening when they insisted that we all go to our bedrooms and give them "privacy."

Once a week, Mama took all of us to the *hamam*—a Turkish steam bath in the Old City which, I was told later, was owned by the Nammamreh. We always looked forward to this wonderful experience not only to get clean but because it was an almost blissful treat to wash with olive oil soap and a *leefa*—a natural plant fiber—creating a soothing massage. The *hamam* had two sections—one for the men and the other for the women. Since I was still very young, around five years old, Mama included me with the women—my first experience with nudity! I was amused watching the women walking somewhat awkwardly in wooden clogs, which were specially made so the women would not fall on the wet floor. Mama didn't offer me clogs because my feet were too small, so I walked barefoot. In traditional Palestinian society, mixing men and women in public places was frowned upon and exclusively reserved to the privacy of the home and among families. In the women's section in the *hamam* there were young, attractive Russian women who gave massages. They had special rooms for women to remove unwanted hair, using the traditional art of wax made with a mix of lemon and sugar.

About once a month on Sunday afternoons, Mama took all eight of us brothers and sisters to the Rex Cinema to see a film for twenty-five piasters, just pennies. The films were in black-and-white and in English, with poor sound quality, but we didn't care and enjoyed them immensely. I loved two films in particular. The first starred Johnny Weissmuller as Tarzan, and his beautiful wife, Jane. We were thrilled to watch Tarzan swim away from dangerous crocodiles, and swing and jump from tree to tree, along with his monkey, Cheetah. After the film we rushed to the forest to pretend to be Tarzan, jumping from one tree to another like monkeys, occasionally coming home with scratches and bruises. The second film I loved was the black-clad, masked Zorro riding on his white horse and heroically fighting evil gangs with his sword. My brothers and I entertained ourselves by imitating Zorro, using wooden sticks as our play swords and slashing the "Z" sign of Zorro on the ground.

One day, right in our backyard, my older brothers Daoud and Suleiman accidentally discovered a deep cave carved inside a huge rock, with steps leading down to the center of a large empty room at the bottom of the rock. It was a mystery we have never been able to solve. We suspected that it was a Roman or Crusader burial, as the tomb inside was designed to resemble a cross. It certainly made a good hideout. Unfortunately, Baba forbade us to enter or play inside the cave, and to scare us he told us that there was a big snake inside protecting the dead. From then on we didn't dare wander in the forbidden cave.

As a child I often played in a beautiful densely wooded forest called H'oursh al-Nammareh—the Nammareh forest— adjacent to the Haret al-Nammareh. I remember Mama and Baba telling me, "Go play in the *h'oursh* and take Laddie for his walk." This was a perfect place to hike, especially in the spring, to pick *za'tar* (thyme) and *snobar* (pine nuts). We picked red and purple poppies (called *hanoon*) and pink, white, and red cyclamen (*qurn al-ghazal*). These beautiful delicate plants were scattered throughout the terraced landscape of Palestine, blooming rainbow colors in spring. On the way back home from the Nammareh forest, I occasionally passed by the lepers hospital in Baq'a. It was surrounded by a high stone wall to keep the patients confined inside. To prevent outsiders from climbing the wall, sharp pieces of glass were cemented all along the top. Occasionally, I climbed the wall to get a glimpse. It was a scary, mysterious place inside.

The Haret al-Nammareh was a unique neighborhood to our extended family. Since our house was large, with two stories, our immediate family lived in the lower level, while our first cousins lived in the upper level, which had its own entrance from the side of the house up a limestone staircase. We visited each other frequently, especially during the holidays. Uncle Rashid had six girls and one boy, all about our ages. They were very friendly and we played together often, and sometimes fought. In the afternoons our mothers visited each other for *qahwah* (coffee) and to help each other cook time-consuming dishes such as *mahshi warak e'nib* (stuffed grape leaves) and *mahshi malfoof* (stuffed cabbage) while waiting for our fathers to return from work. During the warm summer days, we gathered in front of our house with our cousins to play soccer. Sometimes we accidentally tripped each other, falling on the hard black asphalt and running home crying to Mama with a bloody knee. My sisters usually played with the other girls, talking and laughing under our large fig tree.

My oldest sister, Fahima, often helped Mama, particularly with us younger brothers. With eight children, Mama simply didn't have much time to attend to each of us. As Fahima was the closest to Mama, she learned a great deal from her and picked up many wonderful traits. Fahima fulfilled an essential daily role by assisting with cooking, washing dishes, ironing our clothes, and cleaning our home. She became my favorite big sister and she was always there for me. Some of my friends thought she acted as my mother. In a sense she raised me by taking special care of me: feeding and dressing me, and ironing my clothes. This was a privilege at the time, and I appreciated it since I always wanted to look sharp. I also admired her beauty, understanding, and patience. She became an excellent seamstress and sewed her own dresses, so she always looked elegant and beautiful. She also loved music and became a very good dancer.

The last member of our family was our large male dog, Laddie, a handsome, friendly creature with short, shiny, golden fur. He was always underfoot and wanted to follow us to school. In the afternoons, Mama always knew when we were coming home as Laddie would wag his tail, even when we were several blocks away at the bottom of the hill. We regularly competed to take him on walks, and he would follow us everywhere—wherever we played, he wanted to go along. Laddie was my pal, and I often took him along for walks in the forest. We ran happily, chasing each other and playing hide-and-seek. When I felt the urge to pee, I would stand behind a tree and Laddie would stand next to me doing the same. He would lift his leg, while I stood firmly on my two legs, and he would look at me amused. Several trees later, he would wait for me—disappointment on his face, as if saying, "Come on, time to pee." Sometimes when I had to reprimand him, he would bow his head and put his tail between his legs or hide behind a tree. Our outings together created a lasting bond. To communicate, Laddie would look at me with his beautiful honey eyes, making direct eye contact. He would look to me for direction, trusting that I would lead him safely. I knew Laddie was happy by his endless frolicking, smiling, and sparkly eyes. When he was sad he could pout better than any of the children. I could count on his enduring friendship. I felt we would always be there to protect each other.

—

While Baba was away on business, Mama stayed at home, caring for us and perfecting her cooking skills. Mama was a connoisseur of Middle Eastern cuisine. Her cooking techniques were always sought after by our family and friends. She prided herself on improvising and cooking large meals from very simple ingredients, and took charge of the kitchen. She was eager to demonstrate and teach others with her talents. She loved to cook delicious international meals, influenced by Palestinian, Armenian, Italian, and other traditions. Our diet generally consisted of a great deal of fresh vegetables and grains, such as rice, bread, lentils, garbanzos, olives, and plenty of olive oil, with very little meat.

Without adequate refrigeration, each morning Mama descended to the food market to handpick the best fresh vegetables and ripe fruits for that day's meal. Some special meals she cooked only once a year because of the seasonality of certain rare vegetables, and thus we craved these meals when the time came for their preparation. We never understood how she was so well-organized and able to cook time-consuming meals for eight hungry and growing children day after day. But she always encouraged us, especially my sisters, to watch her in action. We all became wonderful cooks. Even some of the boys picked up her talent, particularly Daoud and I, who became good cooks simply by hanging around the kitchen and being the guinea pigs and master tasters of the family!

Occasionally, when not away on business, Baba accopanied Mama to the market to shop for food. He loved to buy in large quantities and always haggled and looked for bargains. For example, during the watermelon and cantaloupe season, he purchased not one, two, or three pieces, but often ten or more. Since there was limited storage space in the kitchen, he would roll the fruits under our beds on the floor. "Here they stay cool and fresh," he insisted. As a result, our family had always an abundance of fruits in our home and under our beds.

Once in a while Baba got in the mood to cook and would take over the kitchen from Mama to make his signature spicy salad. Selecting the biggest, sharpest knife he could find, and acting as a chef, he would chop—into very fine pieces— onions, tomatoes, cucumbers, parsley, mint leaves, and a lot of green hot peppers. He then mixed all the vegetables in a large bowl with black pepper, salt, olive oil, and tahini— sesame oil paste. He would periodically taste it, declaring, "It needs more pepper," adding more, tasting again, and adding more. When he was finished, he had us sit around the table to serve the salad in small bowls with pita bread. The salad smelled very appetizing and tasty to eat. The only problem was that it was so hot that tears would roll down our cheeks and our eyes got red. "It is very healthy for you. Do you like it?" he'd ask. We didn't want to offend him, so reluctantly we ate the whole thing, with large amounts of bread!

As children we grew up eating homemade falafel, hummus, and many other famous Arabic dishes. My mother's delicious *hummus bi-tahini* recipe (chickpeas with sesame oil) was a typical ingredient of the Palestinian diet. It was a thick blend of ground chickpeas and diced garlic, mixed with fresh lemon, parsley, cumin, olive oil, and tahini. Hummus is customarily eaten in a half-loaf of pita bread. This traditional meal was passed from one generation to another among members of our extended family.

I loved the house where I was born. The front yard was spacious, with a large vegetable garden and many fruit trees planted by my grandfather, uncle, and Baba. We had figs, pine, *saber* (fruiting cactus), grapevines, and mulberry trees. In one corner of the yard we raised pigeons, chickens, rabbits, and sometimes sheep that Baba kept. Our home, like others in the neighborhood, had a well that stored the rain for our consumption. We were never hungry; food was in abundance. During spring, at dawn, one could find us on top of the mulberry tree eating the fruit, competing with the many local birds. Mother would wash everyone's mouth and red-stained hands, as she disapproved of our excessive eating. "You will have stomachaches," she often said. Of course, she was right. But our mulberry eating was healthy except for the frequent trips to the outhouse. In summer, we enjoyed eating the fruits of the fig tree that gave us slightly worse results.

As our family grew, more rooms were added to our house. The front entrance to our home was made from solid arched wood framed in iron. We only had one traditional large metal key used for the entire family. As it was impractical for any one person to carry the key, Baba placed an oversized flower pot next to the door with a beautiful aspidistra plant under which we hid the key. It was our "family secret," never mind that many of our friends and neighbors knew about it. Most houses were never locked; by custom, neighbors looked after each other and homes were secure. Life felt simple and authentic. The community was a large family, our collective consciousness was at ease, and our streets were peaceful.

One time I became friends with several *Engleez,* British soldiers, who established their camp in an olive field near Haret al-Nammareh. Sometimes they would take pictures of us while we were playing with our toy guns or hide-and-seek.

At a British Mandate military camp,
defending Jerusalem with a toy gun! (1947)

*My younger brother Zakaria and I with
Scottish soldiers John and Jerry. (1947)*

The soldiers made fun of how we spoke and dressed and often
told jokes about us. In turn, my brother Zakaria and I would
make fun of the fact that some were Scottish and wore kilts,
which to us looked like skirts over bare bottoms. But at times
they allowed me to hold their rifles, and I would pretend I
was shooting at enemies.

Late one afternoon, a friend and I followed two of the soldiers to the H'oursh al-Nammareh. To our surprise we saw an attractive black woman following them. They went to a hideout in the woods. We sneaked up on them and hid behind thick trees. Blissfully unaware of their audience, they undressed completely. We were quite innocent because Baba always insisted against stories that included any hint of sex, out of respect to my sisters.

A comforting memory during the period of the British Mandate was of Mama waking me up each morning by kissing me on my forehead and telling me softly that it was time to get ready for school. Sometimes when Mama was busy preparing breakfast, she would send my sister Fahima to wake me. I loved going to school and the twenty-minute bus ride that brought me there. I would take the number four bus each day from Baq'a to Bab al-Khalil, Jaffa Gate, to the heart of the Old City and then walk to school. Since my father was an associate member of Al-Shareket al-Wataniya, the national bus company, he drove one of the buses and frequently took one of us with him sitting next to him on long journeys. Most bus drivers knew me, and when I proudly announced as I boarded a bus on my way to school that I was "*Ibn Nammamreh*" (son of Nammamreh), the driver would let me ride for free.

After school each day I returned to the bus stop, walking on the smooth cobblestones through the narrow streets of the exciting shopping district, past the crowded Old City's famous Suq al-A'ttarine, the open-air spice market. I watched the women there, some flaunting their new Western clothes with decorative hats, while most dressed in their traditional, colorful, hand-embroidered dresses and scarves. There were large bags of dried beans, burghul, flour, sugar, and spices of many kinds. The sweet and strong smell of cinnamon, allspice, and cloves led to the center of the market where a merchant sipped his strong black coffee while refilling the spice bags. The sounds of intense haggling going on between various merchants and customers drifted through the suq. I was particularly fond of the store that sold tahini, sesame seed paste, and my feet always guided me there. Sometimes I would dip my finger to taste this rich smooth delicacy. The aromas of the market would cling to my body even as I arrived home.

Occasionally I could not resist the temptation of the beautiful displays of fresh fruits and vegetables brought by the *fellaheen,* or farmers, who came each morning at dawn from the many small charming villages surrounding al-Quds. These women walked gracefully, balancing their produce on their heads in baskets handwoven in their villages. My young taste buds were enticed by the pomegranates with their red ruby-like seeds, sweet and juicy. I might pick an apple and run. It was mischievous, but the owners never chased me. Only later did I learn that some of the stores in the suq were also owned by the Nammamreh family, and perhaps that was why they were letting me go.

Often I walked by the coffee, *qahwah,* vendor, a fellow who carried his aromatic, freshly roasted coffee and heavy coffee maker on his back. I also knew Zuzu, a Sudanese peanut peddler who made al-Quds his home when he ran out of money after his pilgrimage to Mecca. Zuzu was a dark-skinned, middle-aged man, a little chubby, with a friendly smile. He always seemed happy and ready to chitchat. Some of his stories were cheerful, and often funny. To earn a living he roasted peanuts in a primitive fire pit. Approaching, I would hear him call loudly, "*Fustuq sukhun, fustuq sukhun, mil wahad, mil wahad*" ("Hot peanuts, hot peanuts, one penny, one penny!"), and I would smell that unmistakable aroma.

Sometimes I stood in line waiting for him to roast a new batch to keep up with demand. When my turn came, I handed him a penny, and for this he would place in the palm of my hand one full scoop of warm, delicious peanuts or drop them onto a piece of torn newspaper and hand it to me with a grin on his face. I would finally get to the bus stop, eating peanuts.

For centuries it had been customary for housewives to pass time in the afternoons by visiting and socializing with our extended family in Haret al-Nammareh in a relaxed atmosphere and discussing family matters. The women would engage in conversation, play cards, and drink thick, freshly ground *qahwah*—Arabic/Turkish coffee with cardamom. It was a symbol of hospitality. As a Turkish proverb says, "A cup of coffee will build friendship for forty years." The coffee is ground in a *tahuni*, a hand grinder made of brass, and brewed carefully in a special pot called a *rakwa*. Brewing *qahwah* is an art in itself, requiring boiling several times, each with special care. Carelessness results in poor taste or in the *qahwah* boiling over; then a fresh brewing is required. *Qahwah* was served in small, delicate cups, usually at the end of the meal. It was black and bitter during sad occasions like funerals, and sweet during happy times such as weddings and festivals. While sipping, each woman made a wish or hope. After drinking, they twirled the cup several times and turned it upside down to pour the sediment into the matching saucer. In gratitude it was customary to say *"Bil afrah"* or *"Daymah"* and the host would answer *"Sahtein,"* short for, "May it bring you good health."

After the cup dries, the grounds form images that are interpreted. Mama learned the magic art of *qahwah* cup fortune-reading through her storytelling and through a lot of experience. The symbols could mean many things: a heart (love), a bird (mail), a road (travel), coins (richness), black (sorrow), white (purity), and so on. When in doubt, King Solomon's wisdom was invoked, with the fortune teller reciting poetic phrases that were as fascinating as the fortune itself, such as the favorite proverb, "*Ba'd al shita' al jaw na'im*" ("After the storm, beautiful weather"), or after sorrow comes happiness.

Neighbors and family members would customarily rotate from home to home to practice their traditions and help each other prepare elaborate dinners for their families, especially during holidays. We always celebrated the holidays, particularly Christmas, New Year's, and Easter. On Christmas, Mama took us to the Church of the Holy Sepulcher in the Old City, and once in a while to Bethlehem's Church of the Nativity, sometimes even to the Midnight Mass. This mass was very long and seemed to take forever, so some of us often slept through it. I always looked forward to Christmas since Baba surprised us with gifts—mostly new shoes, pants, and shirts, not many toys. Mama and my sisters spent many hours cooking our favorite meals and desserts, like *ka'ek wa ma'mool,* or holiday cookies, a Palestinian specialty stuffed with dates and walnuts. On New Year's Day we stayed home; as we were still young, our celebration was relatively modest and peaceful. Mama cooked a large meal, as usual, then we huddled around Baba to hear him recount stories about his interesting and often exotic trips.

I distinctly remember one Easter when after an early dinner we celebrated the ritual of coloring fresh eggs picked from our own chicken coop. Mama boiled the eggs and decorated them using native plants. She used separate pots for each color: dried yellow onion peels for an orange-brown color; *hanoon* (poppies) for a deep pink-purple; beets for red;

and almond-tree leaves for a canary-yellow color. After coloring, it was customary to play a traditional game to determine who had the strongest hard-boiled egg. We each selected one egg. The objective was to hit the top of the other person's egg and crack it, while each of us held our own egg tight in our hand. The person who broke the other egg won and got to keep it. Some would select the biggest eggs believing them to be the strongest. I asked my sister Fahima which she thought was the strongest. With confidence she said, "It is not the size that matters, rather it is the toughness which is important." So I would choose the smallest, most pointed one. After we played, first among ourselves and then with the neighbor's children, I would come back home happy with several eggs in my basket, while my friends were not as lucky.

Baba traveled on business frequently. I remember him choosing my older brother Daoud to go along on a trip with him to the Sea of Galilee (otherwise known as Lake Tiberius). I was a little jealous, thinking how lucky Daoud was, but hopeful that I would get to go on another trip. Upon his return, Daoud was anxious to share his exciting trip with us. Daoud recounted that, as the bus approached and descended towards the lake that afternoon, he was amazed to see the calm blue water for the first time. They arrived at the fishing city of Tiberius (Tabariya) and walked on the promenade along the lake, dotted with open-air restaurants.

Baba seemed to know most everyone, from the restaurant owners to the fishermen that provided the *musht* (Saint Peter's fish). The fresh catch was displayed on ice in front of the restaurant's entrance, and Baba chose a large fish for himself and a small one for Daoud. After dinner Baba introduced Daoud to his fishermen friends who took them sailing on the lake. In the cool evening they went back to the promenade to watch the fishermen prepare their boats for night fishing. They saw three or four boats together light their lanterns and throw their long nets in the water. They could hear them singing and playing the drums to scare the fish into the nets. The boats drifted away in the darkness. The fishermen slept on their boats all night. As the sun was rising in the early morning, the fishermen returned to shore with an abundant catch of *musht*. Daoud told of this magical scene as if time stood still, and it was like the biblical days of two thousand years ago when Jesus walked these same places.

3

A VILLAGE IN THE LAND
OF CANAAN

In Palestine there were once over twelve hundred villages scattered throughout the mountains and countryside, some dating back two to four thousand years. The villagers belonged to the land and were connected to it, physically and spiritually. The shepherds, artisans, and farmers who formed the "bread basket" proudly fed the entire country for many years. Each village was unique, laced with terraced hills that covered the landscape, evidence of a prosperous agricultural history with abundant cultivation of grapes, apples, pears, figs, almonds, pistachios, walnuts, olives, oranges, and many beautiful flowers and vegetable gardens. The richness of village culture was exemplified by the beautiful village of Battir, which blended with the country scene that lay eight kilometers southwest of al-Quds, in the mountains, next to the al-Quds–Jaffa railroad.

The village of Battir (before 1948)

My family's first connection to Battir was inspired by my sister Fahima. The French nuns at Saint Joseph school raised rabbits for their consumption, a French custom. So on the way to school each morning, Fahima would stop at the produce market to pick up scraps of radish leaves, lettuce, and other vegetables to feed the small creatures. As a result, Fahima became good friends with a wonderful *fellaha* (female farmer) named Fatima 'Alayan from the village of Battir who came early each morning to sell her produce. This friendship grew as Mama invited Fatima to our home and gave her hand-me-down clothes. In turn, she gave us fresh fruit baskets and vegetables. Our families became good friends and found common interests. On Saturdays she would come to help mother hand wash the huge pile of our clothes and hang them outside on the clotheslines to dry. White bed sheets bathed in the rays of midday sun and fluttered like a string of peace flags. Mama often asked us to help take down the laundry from our clotheslines, and Fahima would fold them neatly. On holidays and summer vacations, we reciprocated by visiting Battir, a fifteen-minute train ride in the boxcars, which were free for the *fellaheen*.

My experiences as a city boy interacting with this charming village gave me insight into the life and character of Palestinian peasant society. First, hospitality and generosity are two delightful characteristics of the Palestinian *fellaheen*. For instance, Palestinians will borrow money from their neighbors to feed their guests when they are in a bind. But Battir lived in an abundance of foods and produce, though it was short on some luxuries that we in the city took for granted, like indoor plumbing.

In Battir, the tradition was that children always did what their parents did. Men mostly plowed the fields, built homes, and did other strenuous manual labor. Women raised the children, cooked, and cultivated the fields. In turn, adults taught their skills to their children. There was little thought that children might choose to move into other areas of work. They were satisfied with things that way.

The notion of agriculture as a way of life was especially true of Battir. Agriculture, to the *fellaheen,* was not merely a way to make a living but a way of life. Every farming practice had deeply rooted implications that for centuries had been transmitted from generation to generation. One could find tools such as the wooden plow, the hand-grinding stone, and similar ancient household devices. But more importantly, one could also find the stories, beliefs, and attitudes that went with them.

There were no grocery stores or any type of business in the village, not even a bakery. Every house had in its backyard its own *taboon,* an outside oven in which wood is burned and bread and traditional meals are baked. The bread was baked daily, as it had been for thousands of years. The prepared dough was placed on hot stones over burning coals in a small mud hut that retained the heat. Every day one could see smoke rising from each home in the village, creating a mélange of sights and smells. The aroma of bread baking was wonderful, and we children would wait impatiently to get a piece of it, warm, fresh, and delicious.

One memorable weekend in the spring of 1946, our family was invited to the wedding of our friend's daughter in Battir. After our short train ride, we arrived in the early afternoon to a village decorated with flowers, flags, and banners. The parents had decided that their daughter, Wafa, was to marry her cousin, Ali. Apparently, the bride and groom had little to say about it, as their choice of mates also depended upon their parents' wishes. The deals between the two families were agreed upon, the dowry established, and the wedding date set.

We knew and were prepared for the notion that the wedding ceremony would be a three-day affair. The first celebration was on Friday evening at Wafa's home. This party was for women only. Fortunately, however, since I was just five years old, I was permitted to go. The living room was small, and most of the women sat on carpets in a circle or reclined against the wall. I sat on my mother's lap. The women were dressed elegantly in their traditional hand-embroidered dresses and did not cover their faces or heads. They were joyful, talking and laughing. Then the bride entered wearing a colorful, silky, flowing dress and an elaborate headdress adorned with gold and silver coins. I remember thinking that she looked like a princess. All the women clapped their hands and sang as the bride danced in the middle of the room. Everyone agreed that she was a beautiful young bride.

Yet, even though it was special to be part of the women's celebration, I felt out of place with them, so Mama sent me to be with the men. Separately, the men congregated all together at the groom Ali's home, which was just built and attached to his father's house. The men also sat on the floor on carpets, in a circle, with their backs against the wall. The room smelled of smoke; many men were huffing and puffing cigarettes or bubbling on the *argileh,* traditional water pipe. They joked and made fun of Ali, who was a timid young man. There was an assortment of appetizers including *bizer* (watermelon seeds), *fuzduq* (nuts), *qahwah* (coffee), and *shai* (tea*)*. The smoke was getting thick as the evening progressed, so my brother Daoud walked me back to our host's house.

The wedding took place on Saturday, early in the afternoon. All the men and women of the village congregated at Wafa's home to watch as family members helped her onto a white horse. Wafa was dressed in a traditional embroidered wedding dress with a fresh flower wreath on her head. The wedding party processed through the center of the village, followed by the entire community, dancing and singing all the way to Ali's home. The groom was waiting enthusiastically to receive his bride, welcoming her to his modest castle. Then the two families began an elaborate celebration, a joyful festival with plenty of traditional Palestinian foods: the men barbecued whole lambs; the women prepared rice, beans, salads, fruits, and various sweets; and beverages were served— lemonade for the youth and coffee and tea for the adults. It was a memorable wedding for a wonderful young couple.

The care of terraced slopes in Battir, as elsewhere in Palestine, was passed down from generation to generation for hundreds of years. For centuries the immortal *shajarat al-zeitoun*—the olive tree—had become the landscape symbol of Palestinian nationalism. Olives form the backbone of Palestinian agriculture. The olive tree is life, peace, hope, and survival, and we call it the "tree of eternity." The green-gray olive tree has been planted on the land and has given of itself to us for thousands of years. Some trees are over four thousand years old and are called *zeitoun roumani,* Roman olives, because they go back to the time of the Romans. The olive branch, carried by the dove, is a biblical symbol of peace. For most villagers and Palestinians, olives and olive oil are a main source of food, livelihood, and wealth. Great value is attached to orchards with olive trees.

Every season from mid-October through November my family joined in the traditional olive harvest along with other extended family members. Mama would take my brothers, sisters, and me out of school to participate in this ritual of olive picking. The fall olive harvest was a joyous occasion for our family, picnicking and picking the green or purple olives of the year's abundant crop. Later we sat on the ground under the trees cracking open the large, healthier green olives to make *zeitoun mokassar* (cracked olives) to pickle them for consumption for the following year. Mama would stuff the olives in glass jars of water, sea salt, and lemon juice with slices of lemons and a few olive leaves. The remaining smaller olives were taken to presses to produce olive oil—nothing was wasted. Mama humbly explained, "Each olive makes one drop of oil, just like each grape makes one drop of wine."

———

One afternoon on a hot summer day when I was six years old, Mama took me along to visit her friends who lived in the Montefiore Jewish Orthodox housing colony. It was on a hill overlooking the Old City. In it was the largest *marwaha*, a windmill built by Moses Montefiore, a Jewish Zionist, as a landmark to symbolize the early Jewish colony. This was my first exposure to a Jewish colonial settlement.

Our visit seemed to drag on forever. I became impatient because none of the kids would play with me. I remember tugging on Mama, asking repeatedly to go home, but being ignored. Finally, I told her that if we did not leave now, I would go alone. She pretended not to hear me. So I set out walking even though I didn't know the way back home. It was already late in the afternoon. The sun was setting as I headed toward al-Quds railway station. After a short walk, I found the railway tracks. It seemed like a good idea for me to keep walking on the path. I was angry, stubborn, and feeling sorry for myself.

I started to entertain myself by hopping from one railroad tie to another and counting from one to seven, jump double-ties, and then continue. Once in a while I would put my ear to the steel track to hear the train coming. After a few minutes, I heard the whistle telling me that the train was coming directly at me. I would hop off the track, the train rolling by me while I waved to the conductor. I amused myself by counting the train engines and boxcars that went by. Sometimes there were two or three engines attached, which doubled and tripled the number of boxcars, followed by a caboose. I wondered where the train was going, hoping the conductor would stop to give me a ride.

After walking all afternoon without food or water I was hungry and thirsty. Time seemed to have slipped away, and it was getting dark. I heard dogs barking and what sounded like wolves howling. I became scared, realizing that I was lost, and began crying. I decided to get off the track and walk on the gravel road parallel to the railroad.

Fortunately, a *fellaha* riding on her donkey spotted me, stopped, and asked, "Where are you going?" "To Battir," I answered, hoping to play with my friends instead of waiting for Mama in Montefiore. "Where are your parents?" "My mom sent me to visit my friends," I replied. "Alone?" Unconvincingly, I nodded my head. "Yes." She was apprehensive and concerned to leave me alone. "Would you like to ride with me?" she asked.

"Yes, thank you," I replied timidly. "Come here," she said. She lifted me up on her lap to ride along on her donkey.

On our way, I was still crying and thirsty, so she stopped at an *ain*, a natural spring well, to wash my face in the fresh, pure, cold water. She gave me a drink using the palm of her hands. I now felt better and safe in her arms, for she treated me as her child. We finally arrived in Battir late in the evening. Since it was a small village, everyone knew one another, and it was easy for me to locate our friend's home. They were surprised to see me and even more so when I told them that my mother had sent me here for a few days' vacation! They innocently believed me, and as there was no telephone or other means of communicating with my parents, they invited me to stay with them for the whole weekend.

It was wonderful to be away from the city in the healthy climate of the country air, to see the olive trees scattered across the slopes and the grapevines leaning over the terrace walls. Since there was limited space in the one-bedroom house, I was happy to sleep with the boys on the flat roof, watching the myriad stars twinkling in the dark night. The sky was always clear and bright. It seemed we were close to heaven and that we could touch the stars. We counted the stars and got excited watching them fall across the atmosphere. I was awakened in the morning by the rooster's call at sunrise with dew still on my face. My hosts treated me as one of theirs, feeding me homegrown fruits and vegetables, and fresh eggs from their chickens. I loved to eat the delicious *khubz u zeit u za'tar*—fresh bread baked each morning, dipped in olive oil and thyme powder with sesame seeds. Jokingly they claimed it was poor people's food.

I particularly craved *mish-mish* (apricots), one of the most delicious but delicate seasonal fruits that ripen for only a short time and which should be eaten promptly. The remaining fruits not eaten immediately were dried on the rooftop, as were figs and grapes. The proverb "*Bukra fil waqt al mish-mish*" ("Tomorrow during apricot season") reminds us that a slim chance and rare opportunity in life should not be missed.

Each morning after breakfast I rode a donkey, along with my friends and the women, to harvest fruits and vegetables in the fields and *wadis* (valleys). I loved riding the donkey; astride his back I saw nature all around me. Once in a while we would stop the donkey to let a flock of sheep cross the path, herded by shepherds. The donkeys were useful for transportation since the roads were graveled, narrow, and hilly walkways. They were stubborn and seemed to have a mind of their own, especially when they woke up in a lazy mood and refused to follow commands. But they were always good at batting away the flies with their long tails to make our ride more comfortable.

I remember one day my friend E'mad fell off after repeated attempts to ride the donkey. He got mad at me for laughing at him, especially since he landed in the donkey's *khara*, or dung, so he shouted, "I was just getting off this stupid donkey, anyway!" Another boy was riding the donkey backwards, pulling his tail and claiming that it was the mule that had his head on backward and his rear in front! On the way back we stopped to fill the clay jars with more fresh water from their spring and to watch the women carry the jars balanced on their heads. I was enjoying perhaps the greatest time of my childhood. I loved the land, playing with the other kids, and the compassion and tranquility in the village. I admired the decency, dignity, and peacefulness in their way of life and felt as if I could live there forever.

It never occurred to me that back home in Jerusalem, my family was looking for me. Later I learned that Mama had been frantic. She had cried when she couldn't find me in Montefiore. Everyone—my mother and my father, my brothers, sisters, and neighbors—had started looking for me. They filed a missing child report with the police for a search throughout the city. It was a time when families felt unsafe about reports of children disappearing, kidnappings, and turmoil in the city. A rumor even started that I had been kidnapped by one of the Zionist terrorists, which they all feared.

After three days without any trace of me, my brother, Suleiman, told Baba that he had a hunch. So he took the train to Battir and immediately found me there. Without a word, but with tears in his eyes, he hugged and kissed me. He thanked the host family for taking care of me, and we quickly took the next train back to al-Quds. To my astonishment, my whole family was waiting for me. I did not understand or appreciate the excitement and the high emotions everyone expressed. Later that evening Baba gave me the lecture of my life and grounded me for weeks.

4

AN ATTACK ON MY SCHOOL BUS

From the time I was born through my early years, my life seemed to be shielded from the violent turmoil that was then brewing with great force.

As early as 1897, at the First Zionist Conference in Basel, Switzerland, planning had begun to establish a Jewish state on all the land of Palestine from the Mediterranean Sea to the Jordan River. Zionist leader Ze'ev Jabotinsky had declared, "... colonization, even the most restricted, must be ... carried out in defiance of the will of the native population."[5] From the beginning, the Zionist strategy was one of *nikayon*, Hebrew for "ethnic cleansing," of Palestinian natives from their entire ancestral homeland. David Ben-Gurion, the Polish-born executive head of the Zionist Organization, knew very well that to create a Jewish majority he must force the Palestinians out. He admitted as early as 1937, "We must expel the Arabs and take their land . . . I support compulsory transfer. I do not see anything in it immoral . . . The Arabs will have to go, but one needs an opportune moment for making it happen . . ."[6]

On one otherwise routine afternoon, the tranquility of my childhood was shattered when our bus was attacked on our way home from school. As we passed near the Montefiore Jewish Colony, machine gun fire broke out from the hilltop, forcing us to lie on top of each other on the floor of the bus while the driver sped ahead. We were terrified. I knew we had been hit because we heard the screams, crying, and panic of students for the rest of the trip. Upon arrival at Baq'a, we dreadfully discovered that two of our student friends had been killed and many had been wounded. I thanked God that, miraculously, my body had been spared, but I was shocked and spiritually wounded. This experience interrupted my childhood and changed my life forever. From then on we began to ride in a makeshift armored bus in an attempt to protect us from further shootings. My parents, along with the other families in the Haret al-Nammareh, began to impose curfews and new safety restrictions, limiting our schooling, and confining our activities to our neighborhood.

Nammamreh Street became our only playground. There we could still play sports and invented games. Among the most popular were street soccer, slingshot shooting, and rock throwing for the boys and jump rope and hopscotch for the girls. I learned to do the jumping-jack drill with vigor, and once I slipped and fell on the sharp edge of the sidewalk, cutting a deep gash in my forehead. This frightened everyone who saw blood running down my face. That same day my youngest sister, Fadwa, got pushed against the wall while playing and cut her forehead, causing profuse bleeding. It hurt me deeply to see her in pain, and I started crying. When my mother saw both of us crying and covered with blood, she feared the worst, an attack by terrorists, who were now approaching the outskirts of Al-Quds.[7]

On the afternoon of July 22, 1946, my family heard a large explosion and saw towering columns of black smoke on a nearby hilltop overlooking Baq'a. We soon learned that the Zionist Irgun Gang, commanded by the notorious terrorist Menachem Begin, had blown up the south wing of the grand King David Hotel, the most luxurious hotel in Jerusalem, which at the time was under British Mandate administration.

On July 22, 1946, under the leadership of Menachem Begin, the paramilitary gang Irgun Zvai Leumi blew up the prestigious King David Hotel, where my brother Mihran was working.

My brother Mihran (right), who was eighteen, was working at the front desk at the time of the King David Hotel attack. (1946)

The explosion was traumatic for our family, since my oldest brother, Mihran, was working in the hotel at the time as a front desk clerk. His job was to greet the many international dignitaries and influential guests, as he spoke several languages. The eight-story hotel was highly fortified with soldiers, tanks, and barbed wire. Mihran remembers, "Four terrorists sneaked in the northern end dressed as Arab delivery crew with seven milk containers filled with 350 kg of TNT explosives ... The attackers burst into the dining room, where they held me and other hotel staff at gunpoint while they planted explosives." [†]

Fortunately, there were mattresses stacked in an adjacent basement room, so Mihran and his friend thought quickly to shield themselves. "We had just seconds to dive for cover before the complex exploded, destroying the entire southern wing of the hotel." Mihran was fortunate to survive. "Beside me I could see legs—two men's legs. I could see their shoes, their trousers. But the rest of them were smashed."

Later that evening Mihran came home with blood stains all over his clothing from helping the wounded. My parents, brothers, sisters, and neighbors welcomed him with great relief and open arms.

This deadly attack killed ninety-one people and injured over one hundred—mostly British officers, Palestinians, and international dignitaries. The Irgun was the first terrorist organization to introduce powerful explosives into Palestine.

Our family despaired when the new terror phase became a permanent reality. In the early morning of April 9, 1948, news reached us that Begin's Irgun, together with the extremist Stern Gang under the leadership of Yitzhak Shamir—both leaders later became prime ministers of Israel—attacked the 750 Palestinian residents of the village of Deir Yassin just west of Baq'a, massacring 110 men, women, and children, and mutilating their bodies. Another massacre occurred at al-Dawayima village in October 1948, where eighty to one hundred Arab men, women, and children were killed.[8]

In addition to the King David Hotel, Deir Yassin, and al-Dawayima, many other brutal massacres would be committed between 1947 and 1949, claiming the lives of untold numbers of native Palestinians. We were horrified by the intensity of the Zionists' hatred of Palestinians and by their desire to destroy our society.

As these events unfolded around me, even as a child I somehow sensed that my life would change. Yet, I could not understand these horrific acts that had such a traumatic impact on me. I felt fear and anger, and found it difficult to do my homework or go to school. Since al-Quds was in the mountains it was always cold at night, so we had to cover ourselves in thick blankets to stay warm. I had trouble sleeping at night, finding myself curled up in a fetal position and having nightmares.

I remember one particular recurring dream in which I was urinating in my bed, pretending I was connected through a long hose to the toilet to relieve myself while I stayed underneath the warm blanket. Then I would wake up, astonished, in a wet bed. In another vivid dream again I was urinating, connected to the same hose, but this time it led directly to our garden. I was surprised to discover that our roses had died. Every night I was sick to my stomach and my heart felt tired and heavy. I was anxious to wake up in the morning and see the sunrise, hoping to brighten my day. But instead of feeling better, I woke up with a bad taste in my mouth and cruel memories.

The terrorist attacks on Jerusalem also spread to the village of Battir. I was dismayed to learn that the healthy, peaceful way of life in the village would not continue. The consequences to the community were devastating and many of their customs were destroyed. Battir had subsisted primarily from the fruits of the land and from trade with al-Quds. The village became cut off and the villagers made dependent on each other for survival. The hardships disrupted social life. One noticed how the columns of smoke from the old taboon ovens of each family home in the village began to die out one by one.

5

THE DAY BEFORE MY
SEVENTH BIRTHDAY

The day before my seventh birthday, May 15, 1948, was one of the most horrible days of my childhood. That day marked the beginning of *al-Nakba*, the great catastrophe, the exodus of Palestinians from our lands. Zionists had converged on Palestine from all over the world. Through violence they spread panic and terror in the Palestinian population to force us to flee our homes. [9]

That May the rumors of the past months became real threats to our lives. Fear of potential massacres caused eighty percent of Palestinians to escape to neighboring countries. Refugee camps were set up by the United Nations in Jordan, Syria, Lebanon, Egypt, and the remaining Palestinian territories. Palestinians had become refugees for the first time in our history.

Throughout the country, fighting broke out between Palestinian civilians and heavily armed Jewish militias. Soon

Arab soldiers from neighboring Arab states joined the battle, but the Zionist forces had more troops than all the Arab states combined. Arab soldiers were in fact weak, disorganized, ill-equipped, ineffective, and easily defeated. Arab countries still under British or French colonial rule were prevented from joining the war effort. The conflict was not one between equally competing military armies but between heavily armed and trained Zionist paramilitary forces and volunteer Arab fighters who were unprepared to defend their own land.

Al-Quds, the "Eternal City," was transformed into a phantom city. Before the war had even started and a single neighboring Arab soldier had entered Palestine, more than three hundred thousand Palestinians were expelled. Over thirty thousand from West Jerusalem were forced out. Terrorist bombings by Zionists targeted buildings in the city. Ordinary Palestinian citizens took up arms, streets were blockaded.

Zionist militias began to attack the large, middle-class Arab suburbs in West Jerusalem. Our neighbors in Haret al-Nammareh started to flee the highly equipped Zionist militias who had begun advancing toward our neighborhood. Raiding parties cut telephone and electric wires. My father heard the Zionists demand that we all leave immediately. Their loud-speaker-equipped vans drove through the streets, blaring such messages as "Unless you leave your houses, the fate of Deir Yassin will be your fate!"

Even our relatives began to evacuate their homes. They pleaded with my parents that since the terrorists were approaching, our family, too, should leave Haret al-Nammareh, if only for the sake of us children. There were very few Jews living in West Jerusalem in 1948, as it was primarily an affluent Palestinian residential neighborhood.

I vividly remember my father and mother debating what to do. They feared for our safety and security. Yet, Baba insisted that this was our home, and Mama agreed that we must remain *sumud*—steadfast. Instead of fleeing West Jerusalem, we resolved to seek temporary refuge at the German Colony Hospice to protect ourselves from the violence. The Colony encompassed a church, a school, a hospital, and a convent for the nuns, and it was only a fifteen minute walk down the street. My mother was convinced that her longtime special friendship with the nuns would harbor and protect us. After all, for many years they had looked after most of our medical needs at their clinic.

As the sun was setting that afternoon, Mama was baking fresh *khubz*, pita bread, in our backyard cooking oven. Inside she was preparing chicken with rice and *mlukhiyyi*, a green leafy vegetable, along with *warak e'nib*, grape leaves stuffed with meat and rice. Since our home was on a hilltop, from our backyard we could see the advancing armored vehicles closing in on our neighborhood. For our safety, Baba immediately split us up by sending Mama, all the girls, and the youngest boys to the German Colony, leaving him, Mihran, Daoud, and Suleiman behind to follow us a little later when the food was ready.

The walk to the colony seemed endless, as we heard the sounds of bombs and bullets nearby, and felt the earth shake beneath us. We saw the Zionists' armored trucks and troops rushing in all directions, preoccupied and not paying much attention to us.

We walked close together, holding hands tightly. Mama walked quickly, leading the way while keeping little Zakaria close to her. Wedad and Fadwa marched together. Fahima held my hand, dragging me firmly—one step of hers, two of mine. "We must keep pace," she said to me, trailing close behind. *"Yalla imshu, sur'a!"* ("Let's walk fast!") Mama urged. We trembled and cried all the way. Yet, we reached the colony safely, and the nuns welcomed us.

There, other Palestinian families were already taking refuge. Several hours later, to our astonishment, only Daoud and Suleiman arrived at the colony gate, crying. They explained that on the way they were stopped at a street corner by heavily armed men who spoke Yiddish and German—only one spoke Arabic. "Where are you going?" they had asked. Baba had explained that they were going to the German Colony to unite with the rest of our family. After searching and questioning them for an hour, the men allowed only my brothers Daoud, who was fourteen, and Suleiman, who was twelve, to join the family while detaining Baba and Mihran. Before being taken away in a military truck Baba had unsuccessfully pleaded with them to let Mihran go with my other brothers: "He is only seventeen years old and a minor, please let him go!"

We spent many hours in agony waiting without any news and wondering about the fate of Baba and Mihran. The nuns insisted that we stay at the colony before venturing back home to the uncertainties ahead of us. Although the nuns did their best to comfort us, it was very difficult to sleep, eat, or even function normally. Since there were so many families seeking refuge, there were not enough places to sleep other than on carpets and blankets on the cold concrete floor. For an agonizing time we huddled together, hidden from the outside world. We could hear the bombs exploding and gunfire in the surrounding area. Frantically we worried that Baba and Mihran had been caught in the gunfire, and we imagined the worst. We were frightened that our shelter at the colony might be bombed next. It seemed there was no end to the turbulence raging outside. That night we all congregated in the church to pray for Baba and Mihran's safety.

After about a week passed, we reluctantly decided it was time to go back home. Two nuns insisted they come with us for our protection and accompanied us. Even though the streets were deserted and relatively quiet, we were wary as we walked back to our neighborhood. It was our first glimpse of the damage and destruction of buildings and homes.

On arrival we could not believe our eyes. Our home had been broken into and vandalized. Anticipating the war, my father had stocked large amounts of food in the house. It was heartbreaking to find all our food stolen—big bags of rice, flour, sugar, burghul, olives, olive oil, food cans, fruits, and kerosene. The only good surprise was finding our dog, Laddie, wagging his tail, jumping, waiting to lick us and welcome us home. We hugged and kissed him, thankful that he was alive. We only wished he could talk to tell us what had happened!

Even though we were excited to see Laddie safe, Mama was completely outraged at Baba and Mihran being abducted by the Zionist militias and taken to an unknown location. Our family remained in despair. We were now alone, the only family left in the Haret al-Nammareh. All the other homes had also been robbed and looted by the Zionists. We could not distinguish between terrorists and Jewish civilians; they were all dressed in the same khaki street clothes. We saw trucks full of furniture, valuable Persian carpets, appliances, and mattresses being hauled away.

Walter Eytan was summoned by the acting American consul general to observe and to report on the state of one home in Baq'a.

> Every single room in the house had been smashed up . . . It was
> not merely a question of ordinary theft, but of deliberate and

senseless destruction . . . A portrait had been left hanging on the wall with the face neatly cut out with a knife. As we went from room to room I felt more and more speechless and more and more ashamed.[10]

There were reports of rapes and of lootings of rings and jewelry from the Palestinian dead. Systematic looting was not limited to precious jewelry and furniture. A special effort was made to steal Palestinian historic books. More than sixty thousand books were stolen by Jewish authorities in an attempt to destroy Palestinian culture. Documenting the great book robbery of 1948, journalist Arwa Aburawa later wrote:

Between May 1948 and February 1949, librarians from the Jewish National Library and Hebrew University Library entered the desolate Palestinian homes of west Jerusalem and seized 30,000 books, manuscripts and newspapers alone. These cultural assets, which had belonged to elite and educated Palestinian families, were then "loaned" to the National Library where they have remained until now. The books were later marked with just two letters: "AP" or "abandoned property."[11]

Throughout this time, Mama tried her best to keep us calm and safe. At night she covered the windows with blankets and told us to stay away from them for fear of being harmed. We all huddled together in the corner of a small room like a litter of puppies guarded by their loving mother.

During the day, though, it was hard for Mama to keep us boys inside. Daoud, Suleiman, and I began venturing outside to play and to explore the deserted neighborhood, scavenging for food, which had become scarcer day by day. Sometimes my sisters followed us. For weeks we behaved like wild animals, roaming around freely from one house to another without permission. We had no real supervision or fear of reprimand as Baba was not there to discipline us. Instead we jumped from one yard to another picking figs, mulberries, apples, grapes, and whatever else we could find. We made it a habit and joked about having our breakfast each morning on one of our cousin's fig trees.

Mama became concerned about our behavior, especially when one day Suleiman came home with a live chicken he had caught in one of the neighbor's yards. He simply said he was hungry and asked Mama to cook his favorite dinner—*dajaj mahshi ma' ruz*—stuffed chicken with rice. Even though Mama was apprehensive about Suleiman's behavior, she cooked the delicious dish just as his heart desired.

One afternoon, Suleiman and I saw a Jewish gang looting one of our cousin's home. They saw us and began chasing us. We ran home, jumping over fence after fence. On one of the last fences my groin got caught on a sharp wire, cutting me between my legs. I ran home to Mama hurting while blood was running down inside my pants. She looked at me with shock and decided to rush me immediately to the nuns at the German Hospice. Without any transportation available, Mama and Suleiman carried me as fast as they could.

At the Hospice, two German nuns quickly undressed me to examine my injury. Without showing much emotion, the nuns began to mumble in German between themselves while cleaning my wounds. Mama and I couldn't understand what they were saying. We watched them with concern and worry. One nun finally said, "*Oh no, das ist nicht gut?*" "*Ya, Ya,*" responded the other nun. Apparently, they were concerned about stitching me. At the Hospice, as there were no doctors, the nuns made all the decisions. After serious deliberation they decided to tape the cut to hold the skin together to cover my *bedati*, or testicles, and hope that the wound would heal. Mama later told me that she could see my testicles exposed inside the deep cut. With a scar as a reminder, I reflect back on how much worse the outcome might have been. I am certain that God must have listened to the nuns and Mama's prayers!

One night Daoud, Suleiman, and I sneaked into Villa Rosemary, with bombs and bullets flying all around us. An abandoned small garden hotel adjacent to our neighborhood, it was a popular social hangout for British soldiers and their friends. We stumbled upon a bar fully stocked with liquor. Innocently, we sampled the variety of bottles. Some were juicy, some were sweet and then sour, or some were dry. Of course, after a while we could not tell the difference. We all got drunk and eventually crashed on the hard cold tiled floor snuggled next to each other all night long. In the morning, we dragged ourselves home, smelling like a brewery. Although Mama was very relieved to have us back safely, she was exasperated and bewildered at our reckless behavior during such dangerous times. But we were too young to fully understand the threat surrounding us. Instead, as children, we looked for ways to entertain ourselves and lift our spirits.

As living conditions grew more precarious, however, Mama also had difficulty keeping us healthy, especially trying to prevent lice from invading our hair. One day she decided to cut all the boys' hair short and since there were no barbers, she decided to do it herself using an antique hand-held manual shaver we owned. Without any objection each of us got a short, clean haircut, leaving us to resemble bald-headed old men. Only Daoud refused to have his hair cut as he prided himself on his neatly groomed, long black hair. To add insult to injury, he began making fun of us, calling us *ras ar'a*—"bald heads." Naturally, we did not take this lightly and soon took our revenge. One night when Daoud was sleeping, Suleiman, Zakaria, and I jumped onto his bed. While two of us held him down, Suleiman quickly ran the shaver through the middle of his hair. This made a streak down the center of his head, leaving him with a double-mohawk. He then looked worse than we did and eventually cut all his hair off, too.

The hair cutting episode behind us, our close friendship and dependence on each other strengthened our relationship as brothers. A few days later, on one hot and humid Friday late afternoon, Daoud, Suleiman, and I were playing on the first floor of a vacant four-story building. We heard a big explosion upstairs, followed by continuous loud whistling and banging noises that lasted for several seconds. We decided to creep upstairs to explore. On the fourth floor, in the middle of a large room, we found an unexploded missile, still spinning. It had penetrated the wall of the building and circled the room, destroying all of the furniture. The missile was very hot, so Suleiman found a blanket to wrap it in and take it home for a souvenir.

Realizing what Suleiman had brought home snugly wrapped in a raggedy blanket, Mama demanded that we get rid of the missile right away. She took it, along with Baba's antique hunting shotgun given to him by his father, and buried both of them next door in our neighbor's yard. Her concern was to keep the gun away from us in the hope that none of her children might entertain the crazy idea of joining the fighting and getting ourselves killed, as many other young Palestinians had begun to do. But Mama's fear kept bothering her, so a few weeks later she gave both the gun and the missile to a Jewish soldier who explained to her that the missile was still live and could explode at any time. Mama was relieved and thankful. "God was watching over us," she sighed.

6

CONFINED TO PRISON ZONE A

One day several Jewish soldiers came with a bunch of armed men to our home. They showed up under the pretense that they wanted to help us. They insisted that it was no longer safe for us to stay in Haret al-Nammareh and demanded that we relocate to another neighborhood. They said it was for our own protection, that it would be "only for a few days" and that we would be back "soon." My spirit sank. After futile argument, my mother and all of us seven young children locked our home, secured the key, and against our wishes left our home. All we took were the clothes on our backs and a few personal belongings; everything else we left behind.

At that moment we realized that we were the last of the Nammamreh family to leave our neighborhood. We were escorted to Upper Baq'a and placed in a vacant, dilapidated apartment building still under construction next to the railway tracks. When a train went by it was so noisy it shook the house.

We quickly discovered that we had been forced under military administration law into a fenced security zone (Zone A), confined with Palestinian families from other neighborhoods who had also stayed in their homes. There were also Greeks, French, Italians, and British, both Christians and Muslims. The military zone was a ghetto and a large open prison camp, surrounded by eight feet of barbed wire, with armed guards preventing anyone from leaving or entering. There was no communication with the outside world. We were free to move around in the zone during the day but we were under strict curfew at night. Innocently, we all presumed that this was a temporary arrangement and that we would return to our homes soon, since we all had locked our doors and saved our keys.

Since we had remained in West Jerusalem, under the violently racist ideology of this new regime, we became a minority under siege and an extension of war. We were innocent young children, yet we had to learn to survive as individuals. We measured our ability to sustain ourselves by the way we supported each other and stayed strong as a family.

Our apartment building in the zone was designed to have two or three stories, but only the first floor was completed. The staircase leading up to the second floor was half-finished, with no rails. The lower level was divided into three small apartments, each with three small bedrooms and one old bathroom. Three families lived next to each other. Since the building was still under construction, there were no carpets, tiles, or window finishes. Initially there was no electricity or water piping. As space and furniture were limited, we slept in cramped rooms, two on each bed, and some of us had the luxury of sprawling on the floor. One of my worst experiences

Left to right: (front) Zakaria with our dog Laddie, Mama holding a cat; (back) Fadwa holding her doll, Fahima, and Wedad, in the zone. (1948)

was going to the bathroom and waiting in line every morning behind a large family. The toilet was in the old European style, the squatting type without a seat and toilet paper. We washed with a water bucket. The bathtub was a large copper bowl, and the water was heated in a tin container over a kerosene burner. Mama would mix hot and cold water with soap to pour over our heads, then some water would be reused for the garden. Bathing was limited to once a week.

We were ashamed to live in this place and to bring friends to visit us. The streets became our playground once more. Since there were no schools, we did not need desks, books, or anything usually associated with childhood. The summers were very hot, with open windows our only way to cool the air. This invited dirty biting flies by day and nasty stinging mosquitoes at night. The winters were very cold, as we had no central heating. To stay warm, we had a domestic kerosene stove that we moved from one room to another. Each evening Mama would bundle us with blankets in one room around the stove. For entertainment, Mama roasted peanuts on the stove and told us stories to keep us occupied.

Sometimes Wedad would recount a humorous story of Juha, an ancient beloved comic legend who appeared in various Arab popular literary anecdotes. One day, Juha's wife asked him to go to the vegetable market to buy her a *batinjan*, an eggplant, for supper. "What is a *batinjan*?" asked Juha. "You're stupid!" she told him. "Just think of a man in a navy suit with his head wrapped in a green *tarbush* headdress." "Okay," said Juha. He proceeded to the market looking for such a man. After some searching he found a man who looked just as his wife described. He convinced the man to come with him, saying, "My wife needs you to come home with me." Upon arriving at home, the wife was astonished and asked Juha, "Who is this man and where is the *batinjan*?" Juha replied confidently, "This is exactly what you commanded." "You are both *hameer*—jackasses," she yelled at them.

Furious and hysterical, she chased both of them out of the house with her broom. Such stories made us laugh, even if it was just for a while.

In the zone we went from living a normal life to a dire state of poverty, unsure of when or from where our next meal was coming. To survive, we became completely dependent on charity distributed by the United Nations Relief and Works Agency, who doled out basic food rationing. I remember watching Mama standing for hours in long lines to receive bags of flour, rice, olives, sugar, and, on occasion, canned foods. Since we were a large family, and food was scarce,

Mama had to ration each meal by dividing the food into equal portions among us. We were always hungry to eat her modest cooking and scrape up the food from our plates. No one dared to throw any food away; she would remind us of the poorer people around the world who were starving and that God would punish us if we were wasteful.

Mama regularly sent us scavenging to pick wild dandelions from the field as a substitute for lettuce, to feed us a poor man's salad. On many days our diet consisted of bread, olives, and water, or bread with tomatoes and onions, or bread with olive oil dipped in *za'tar* or sprinkled with sugar. We all were thin and looked like we had not eaten for a while. A major concern was to keep our health, so Mama gave each of us one tablespoon of fish oil each day that the UN had provided, which tasted awful but kept us well.

My mother Tuma (third from right, with handbag), in the Baq'a prison zone, waiting in line for food rations from UNRWA. (1948)

One day a dark, handsome Palestinian man about my father's age and wearing a dirty work uniform knocked at our door. He said he was from Jaffa and a good friend of Baba. He had heard of Baba and Mihran being in a Jewish prison. He knew all about the Nammamreh family, especially our orchards in Jaffa, and said he was very sorry and that he sympathized with our family's conditions. He was a railroad engineer running the train on the Jaffa-Jerusalem route. Since we lived next to the railway track close to the station, he started bringing us fruit from our old orchards.

A week later and every week thereafter, as the train passed our house he honked three times to alert us and then dropped off one or two large sacks full of fresh oranges, grapefruits, and tangerines. Fifteen minutes later he would walk to our house to visit us for a few hours while his train was being prepared for the journey back to Jaffa. For this wonderful generosity all he wanted from us was to provide him with an *argileh* (water pipe) for a relaxing smoke. We happily obliged. He often talked about the beautiful city of Jaffa and the abundant orchards there. He insisted we eat all the oranges he brought to us and explained how healthy they were for us. When we were thirsty he told us, "Take an orange and make a hole at the stem, then squeeze it with both hands to suck the juice in your mouth." It was refreshing and delicious. He also taught me how to peel an orange and a grapefruit all around with a knife, keeping the skin in one whole piece, something I still enjoy doing to this day.

I remember that during this period in my childhood I never received a toy, not even during holidays. My present on Christmas was one set of used clothes, donated by the UN—a shirt, a pair of pants, and shoes that hurt my feet as they did not fit right. All my clothes were hand-me-downs, some twice over from my older brothers, or donations from charity organizations. Even though they were secondhand, it was exciting to receive these gifts. My older sister Fahima became an expert in sizing the clothes to fit me, though at times they were a little baggy. When I occasionally lost a button on my shirt, she would patiently sew on another one. But rarely could she find a matching one, so the buttons were a mish-mash of colors and sizes.

The clothes we most looked forward to were those that Mama either hand-knitted or crocheted. She made sweaters, mittens, hats, scarves, and socks. We felt special when it was our turn to receive one of these handcrafted items. She was so skilled at her work that she didn't need to look at the needles while weaving the yarn. Mama would talk and tell stories while knitting. She said it was relaxing and a good way to pass the time. My sisters Fahima and Wedad benefited by helping her, and in turn they also became very good knitters. Sometimes Mama would reuse old sweater yarns to knit beautiful new ones. We each felt grateful when it was our turn to receive one of these items handcrafted with so much love.

One gloomy afternoon I asked Mama why she was so sad. At first she did not want to talk, but upon my insistence she confided in me saying, "*Habibi,* darling, Ya'coub, my heart is broken. I am horrified about Baba and Mihran's disappear-ance. My memories about the Armenian massacre, my family, and childhood are being repeated again in al-Quds. It is haunting me, and I am afraid that the Zionists are commit-ting crimes against the Palestinians as the Turks did against the Armenians. They are killing us, stealing our homes, our land, and our future." Then her voice filled with emotion. "What I am going through now are the worst days of my adult life. When I was very young in Armenia I used to live in my own home safely and happily. Now I am losing everything. The Zionists, just like the Ottomans, don't have any *dameer* (conscience)." I tried to comfort her, but all I could do was to hug her. I saw in her eyes the pain of dislocation and daily humiliation.

One evening soon after this conversation, Mama was very depressed and needed her spirits lifted. Since it was getting late and the curfew was upon us, we decided it was a good time to play cards to relax and pass the time. *Basra* is an easy-to-learn, old, traditional two-person game. The cards are dealt four each, alternately played, with the highest cards winning. The jack is the most valuable, because with it one is able to collect all the cards, and it offers a second opportunity for a *Basra*, which counts for ten points. Fifty-one total points wins the game. It requires good concentration, memory, and some finesse. The game is entertaining but cannot involve gambling or betting, which are considered *haram*, or forbidden, under Islamic law. Mama often let us win when we were young, but now I felt that she should win. It was wonderful to see her winning, a moment of earlier, happier times.

There were no jobs, schools, or organized activities for children, so most of us played in the streets and generally misbehaved. In the streets we saw tanks, armored trucks, and soldiers with guns, which exposed to us the evils of war. Our pastimes were shooting marbles, playing soccer, and roaming the streets to scavenge for bombs, hand grenades, shells, and bullets, especially live ones. Not everyone survived this pastime; the unfortunate became casualties of history, while others were just lucky.

We never joined the military, engaged in violence, or fought in the war. Instead we passed the time perfecting our skills catching flies, something Palestinians are very good at.

I once asked my older brother Suleiman, "How is it that you are so good at catching flies?" He boasted, "This is an art of quick hands and a lot of practice." "The trick," he continued, "is that you should attack the fly directly from the front with an open palm, snapping it as it takes off forward, not allowing it to fly backward or sideward." It worked, and sometimes he snatched two or three flies in one pass. When he missed, our faithful dog Laddie was there to quickly oblige. But Suleiman warned me, "You know, these flies are vicious. They bite, carry germs, and are a pest." I often wondered about the relevance of catching these flies; perhaps it was the challenge of getting rid of these annoying bugs that were always busy invading our space.

Another major pastime was to make our own slingshots from oak trees. We would select the best Y-shaped branch, cut it to size, and file it smooth. We then searched for scraps of bicycle rubber tubing to make the sling. We practiced hard to master the art of accurate slingshot shooting. Sometimes we missed, hitting our own thumbs. Eventually we became experts, using small rocks to hit targets accurately, especially moving objects. Once in a while we would break a window. Sometimes our play would degenerate into fights that resulted in injuries. On one occasion I was hit on my forehead and the wound left a permanent scar, which became a reminder of my life in the zone and of playing war games. The slingshot and rock became our weapon for protection and a symbol of resistance.

As food was in short supply, my brothers and I started using our slingshots to hunt pigeons and birds, as they were abundant. We liked to sit quietly under a large fig tree waiting for the birds to come, pretending to be great hunters. Most of the time we came home empty-handed, but once in a while we shot two or three poor little creatures, which were in fact more bones than meat. Occasionally, we got lucky enough to bring home one fat pigeon. Mama and my sisters were very angry with us and wanted nothing to do with this, even if we starved. They particularly insisted that we not hunt or harm the *bulbul*, a small festive songbird native to Palestine and a symbol of life and melancholy. When a person sings beautifully, they are compared to this bird, "*beghani zai al-bulbul*" ("they sing like a *bulbul*"). It was refreshing to wake up each morning listening to the *bulbul*'s warbling voice brightening our day and giving us hope.

One Friday night while we were sleeping soundly, we were awakened harshly by pounding on our front door. Rushing to the door, Mama recognized the two Jewish soldiers standing outside. They were the Ashkenazi soldiers who guarded the zone and who spied on us. From time to time they would sneak through the fence to visit, bring us some food, and pretend that they were kind and wanted to help us. We had nicknamed the leader, who had a spotted face and a long, bald, melon-shaped head, *Abu Rassain*—"the man with two heads."

Abu Rassain and his partner were armed and drunk. It was late at night, and we were frightened. We knew they hadn't come on a friendly mission. "We want Fahima to come with us!" they ordered. She was sixteen years old. Mama stood firm. "Under no circumstances you will take or touch her." "She must come or we will take her by force," they shouted. "Are you threatening us? Get out—now!" Mama demanded. We seven children began crying. After an exhausting and lengthy argument Daoud, who was fourteen, stepped forward and placed himself between the gunmen and my sisters. The gunmen stuck their rifles in Daoud's stomach. "Step aside, move," they ordered. "You will have to shoot me first before you touch any one of us," Daoud said assertively. It was a tense stalemate. I remember Mama holding me and hiding my face from the soldiers. Miraculously, with God's divine intervention, they turned and disappeared in the darkness, and we never saw them again.

A week later, in the early morning as the sun was rising over the zone, four Shin Bet officers from the Israeli Secret Police came to our house to falsely accuse Fahima of killing a Jewish soldier. They offered no evidence, names, or information. After a troubling interrogation and harassment, the officers left without further incident. On other days, we had seen the Shin Bet come in the middle of the night to take our neighbors, handcuffed and blindfolded, away from their homes. We never knew why they were taken, and some never returned. We assumed that they had been deported.

The harassment continued when one afternoon Wedad was walking home near the German Colony. An armored truck driven by an Israeli soldier tried to run her down. She ran for her life, jumping and climbing a barrier wall to escape as the truck scraped the side of the wall and sped away. Two nuns came to her aid after witnessing the horror.

I am reminded of a story from the Palestinian family of an old man who lived alone in the zone. The old man wanted to dig his potato garden, but it was very hard work. His only son, who would have helped him, was in an Israeli prison. The old man wrote a letter to his son and mentioned his predicament. Shortly, he received this reply. "For HEAVEN'S SAKE, Dad, don't dig up that garden, that's where I buried the GUNS!" At four o'clock the next morning, a dozen Israeli soldiers showed up and dug up the entire garden without finding any guns. Confused, the old man wrote another note to his son, telling him what happened and asking him what to do next. His son's reply was, "Now plant your potatoes, Dad. This is the best I can do for you now."

As a young child in the zone, time seemed unreal. There were no schedules or deadlines. I just existed. I was consumed with constant fear and the struggle to survive. My heart ached from missing Baba and Mihran, and waiting for their return. Mama tried every day to find out news about them. She went to the United Nations Relief Agency and asked the Jewish soldiers who guarded the zone. They knew that Baba and Mihran were held in a Jewish prison, yet they ignored her. We despaired, not knowing what was happening to them and fearing the worst.

I wanted my life to be simple and safe. I couldn't rationalize what was happening. I was ashamed of the cruelty they inflicted on us. We did not deserve to live such a life. What had we ever done to them?

7

REUNITED: KEEPING OUR FAMILY TOGETHER

A terrible consequence of the conflict was the division of the City of Jerusalem in two: East Jerusalem, which became part of the West Bank and Jordan, and West Jerusalem, which was controlled by Israel, with a "no man's land" running from north to south between the two cities. Palestinians—Christian and Muslim—were prohibited from returning to West Jerusalem, even though they owned most of the homes and land there. Israeli Jews were kept out of East Jerusalem. Most Palestinian inhabitants fled or were forced to move—east, north, south, and far beyond.

Rochelle Davis reminds us that people lost more than their homes and belongings. They also lost

> their businesses, livelihoods, contact with neighbors, friends, nearby village neighbors, and relatives . . . a way of life. The center of Jerusalem social life for the upper middle-class—the

clubs, cafes, and restaurants of the New City—was now out of their reach, as were many of the educational institutions. [12]

As I look back, my family and I were somewhat fortunate to have remained in West Jerusalem instead of ending up in a refugee camp—the fate of most Palestinians. Because Israel refused to allow Palestinians the right of return, the United Nations Relief and Works Agency had to take on the responsibility of caring for the new refugees who had been placed in crowded security camps—first in tents, then in tin or cardboard shacks, and later in shelters made from concrete blocks. There was sporadic electricity and no indoor plumbing for water; raw sewage ran between the tightly packed houses. With only minimal furniture they slept, sat, and ate on the floor and depended on humanitarian aid for survival.

At the same time, newly immigrated Zionists were living in luxurious Palestinian homes on Palestinian land. Our family watched in bewilderment as these events unfolded. More disturbing was to see thousands of new foreigners converge on our city. Since we chose to remain, we became the only Nammamreh left in our neighborhood and among the very few Palestinians who stayed in the western part of the city. In this new Israeli state we became a minority in our own land, completely cut off from the Old City and from the rest of Palestine.

Two and a half years after the State of Israel was established, the prison zone was dismantled. Undermining our rights as citizens, we were issued a *Teu'dad Zehut*, identity card, by Israel's Ministry of Interior. Printed in Hebrew and Arabic, this ID differentiated Jews from Palestinians. It included a picture with your signature, first and family names, the names of your father and mother, your date of birth, religious ethnicity, height, eye and hair color, city, and home address in the zone. The objective of the ID was to privilege Jewish citizens over Palestinians. Aided by the passage of over thirty laws, with this ID we were targeted by government officials who could discriminate against us when we sought access to our land and homes, to employment, or to education.

After receiving our papers, my family's first instinct was to move back to our own home in Haret al-Nammareh where we belonged. But when we arrived in our old neighborhood we were astonished to discover that our home was already occupied by two new Jewish families from Eastern Europe who spoke only Yiddish. They considered us strangers and would not allow us back inside. After agonizing among ourselves for several hours, we were informed by a Jewish soldier, who was stationed outside the house to protect them, that our home had been given to them by the government and that they would not leave. The government had told them that our home belonged exclusively to them and that it had not been expropriated illegally from our family. The soldier explained, "These people believe that God promised them this land, so they came from Poland to claim it."

A week later we protested to the authority, but they advised us that under the newly promulgated 1950 property law we were now classified as and considered "Present Absentees," the same status as "Absentee Land Owners" and "Internal Refugees." The law states that "land and homes left behind by Palestinians as of November 29, 1947 are deemed 'enemy' property and are liable for expropriation by Israel authorities." Even though we had remained, had in fact never left our neighborhood but continued to reside inside West Jerusalem, our home was now considered to be Israeli land dedicated exclusively for use by Jews. With Baba and my oldest brother Mihran still in an Israeli prison, there was little

Mama or any one of us seven young children could do to defend ourselves, or our rights. We had no money to seek legal representation or any way of obtaining justice in the heavily biased Zionist courts. Israel was erasing Palestine, wiping out and changing the names of our cities, villages, neighborhoods, and streets, and covering the ruins of our history with Hebrew names.

We realized that we did not have a home or a place of our own anymore. We had lost not only our own home and possessions but the entire Haret al-Nammareh, seemingly overnight, and become foreigners in our own country. Like hundreds of thousands of other Palestinians, we had been denied our legal right to return to our home, or to receive any compensation.

Years later we would be informed by a UN official that our land title deeds had been registered with the Ottoman archives in Turkey and with the British Government Land Registry in England.

But we saved our key, which over time evolved into the symbol of our home. Today, our neighborhood is one of the most affluent districts in West Jerusalem. Our home, which would have been mine and my children's inheritance, has increased greatly in value.

Disappointed and demoralized, we were forced to return to the zone area in Upper Baq'a to live in the same pitiful place. Our attention and efforts now concentrated on locating Baba and Mihran. To our surprise, Mihran was released in 1951, three years after he had been abducted to prison, to rejoin our family. Apparently he was no longer considered a threat or harmful to the new state. Baba, on the other hand, who was sick and weak, was not released. Instead he was deported across the new armistice border to Jordan in a prisoner exchange.

*Papa and Mihran were detained in Israeli black hole prisons for two
and a half years. Mihran (center) is pictured here. (1948–1949)*

Mihran recounted his long ordeal after he and Baba were
apprehended by Zionist gangs:

> First, we were both blindfolded and taken by armored cars to
> detention at the nearby Neve Shaanan Kibbutz camp . . . along
> with other wounded Palestinians brought from all over the city.
> The prison conditions were terrible. Many detainees suffered
> from bad coughs, vomiting, nausea and high fever—they were
> sick and had very little medical attention. After three months
> one early morning, we were split up and transported. I was
> moved north to a prison in Hertzellya, and Baba was taken with
> other men further north to Atlit, in Galilee, to an old British
> Mandate high-security prison. [†]

Prison life was extremely difficult and disorienting for
both Baba and Mihran since they had nothing to do with the
war in the first place. They were nonviolent and peaceful, not
soldiers, terrorists, militants, or insurgents. Baba had lost a

lot of weight and was eventually bedridden while in prison. On the other hand, Mihran had gained a lot of weight. He had been assigned to kitchen duty as a result of meeting a Jewish acquaintance who had previously worked with him at the King David Hotel and was now an officer. Mihran explained, "I ate a lot of food and got fat because of my anxiety and unpredictable future." As Mihran was one of the few prisoners who spoke Hebrew and Arabic fluently, he became a contact between the soldiers and the other inmates. He became popular with the Palestinian prisoners by providing them with extra food, especially those who were sick and weak.

After Mihran recovered from the prison ordeal, he went back to work at the King David Hotel as a concierge. Later, Daoud joined Mihran at the hotel working as a bellboy and an elevator attendant. On one elevator ride, Daoud befriended an American, Major General William Reilly, the United Nations Chief of Staff, who was staying at the hotel. He invited Daoud to come to his suite later that evening to explain our father's situation, how Baba had been separated from our family and was living in the West Bank alone. General Reilly was touched by Daoud's story and volunteered to assist our family. We heard that he personally called Prime Minister David Ben-Gurion, who within forty-eight hours arranged to bring Baba back from Jordan to reunite with our family.

Baba was escorted by United Nations peacekeepers through the Mandelbaum gate, a demilitarized no man's land and the only legal crossing separating the West Bank and Israel. When he finally arrived home, Baba was relieved and heartened to be back with all of us. About five years had elapsed since we had seen him last. It was a great relief to have our family united once more.

But the ordeal weighed heavily on us. Baba had been a healthy, strong man before he was taken to prison. Now he was thin, sickly, and depressed by what had happened to him, to our family, and to the Palestinian people. From then on he was never the same, and the incarceration had a drastic effect on his well-being.

Baba seldom discussed politics, but one afternoon while we tended the garden he confided in me about the betrayal and double-dealings of the British Government. He blamed them for our loss and for the Palestinian catastrophe, referring to them as "corrupt and traitors." He believed that "they gave Palestine to the Zionists for political gains and guilt" and that the Ottoman Turks did not betray the Palestinians in this way, insisting, "The shoe of the Palestinian *fellah* is more honorable than the King of Britain." He counseled me, "Remember, for every one hundred honorable men, there is always one who is evil . . . you must stay away from that one."

After being released from prison, my father was out of work and most of my brothers and sisters were idle. Israel had stripped us of our ability to earn a living and of any opportunity for a prosperous future. Conditions were getting worse each day, but we were determined to support each other and labor diligently to keep our family together. We did not have much, but we did have each other.

8

SCHOOL YEARS

As time passed by, and two and a half years were wasted in idleness, the childhood I had enjoyed became gloomier as I realized that I would no longer be able to see my school, my friends, or my teachers in the Old City. I had to face the fact that my ties to the Old City, once so much a part of my daily life, had to be given up for some time—if not, a long time. I realized that I would miss sitting by the sidewalk listening to the wise old men as they philosophized and discussed politics. I would no longer be able to hear the Old City church bells each day or to follow the Stations of the Cross behind the annual procession of the Way of the Cross as I used to from the Pontius Pilates Court residence through the Via Dolorosa and into the Holy Sepulcher.

I vividly remember walking to my old stomping grounds in Haret al-Nammareh wondering what my life would have been like if I still lived in my home. I saw a lot in my neighborhood that I could not make sense of. My birthplace was in front of my eyes, but I could not go in. Strangers lived inside.

One spring afternoon, I walked by a small shoeshine and repair shop on a street corner belonging to an old man named Aziz. He, too, seemed lonely, working by himself, pounding nails, repairing used shoes for poor Palestinians like himself who could not afford new ones. He saw me wandering around and asked me to sit next to him on a wooden stool. He was happy to have some companionship and someone to listen to his story as a successful businessman before the war. He saw that I had nothing better to do and so he suggested, "I would like to offer you a job for Palestinian *mils* [pennies] and free history lessons." That day I became a shoeshine boy and was excited to run home after work to show everyone my earnings, which I have saved to this day. The coins were made from heavy brass with a hole bored through the middle, engraved with "1927 *Filastin*" on one side in Arabic, Hebrew, and English; and with "*20 mils,*" also in these three languages, on the other side.

Aziz affectionately named me *Ya'coube*, my little Jacob, and I in return called him *Ya Azizi*, my dear friend. Every morning and early afternoon, he offered me c*hai bil na'na' bil sukar, bidun halib*—tea with fresh mint and sugar, without milk. He insisted that tea with milk was for the British aristocracy only. He despised the British, so to release his anger he sarcastically would spit on the shoes while buffing them to give them a better shine. But Aziz also taught me humility and to be able appreciate the simple things in life. He was proud and wise, a good storyteller, and a self-made philosopher on tradition and life's simple pleasures. Our friendship allowed me to dream and have some hope to cope with the miserable conditions that we were both experiencing.

Next door to Aziz's shoe shop, a Palestinian family began to refurbish a bakery damaged by the war. It was a mom-and-pop bakery primarily for pita bread, run by the husband, his wife, and their two older daughters. One day the father asked me to help him clean the narrow oven. It was about sixteen inches high, four feet wide, and six feet deep. It was impossible for an adult to squeeze in and clean, so he asked me to crawl inside the tunnel-like, pitch-black oven. He gave me a dustpan and a small hand broom to sweep the dirt. When the pan was filled, I handed it to his wife to empty and return back to me. I continued this method of cleaning for several hours. While inside the oven, I imagined the intense heat from the fire coming from the top while the bread was being baked, and what a fresh-smelling aroma it was. I was preoccupied, and so I never thought of, or feared, being suffocated from the soot going into my eyes, face, and lungs. When I finished, all my clothes were covered in ashes and I was coughing black dust. I concluded that it was a hard task for a child, maybe also dangerous, but I was proud of myself. When I finished, they washed my face and hands and complimented me for a job well done. Since money was scarce, they rewarded me with a supply of fresh-baked bread each day for one week to give to my whole family.

During the war while living in the zone, we missed going to school for more than two and a half years. So we were fortunate that, after the war, the Catholic Church opened two schools in West Jerusalem for Palestinians. One was Saint Joseph, a French nun's school for girls that my sisters attended; the other was Terra Sancta ("Holy Land") College for boys, where my older brothers went. But since my younger brother Zakaria and I were still quite young, we were permitted to attend the girls' school along with my sisters and later transferred to the boys' school. The students were mostly Palestinian Christians and Muslims. There were also several students from the diplomatic corps—British, French, and American. I fancied a beautiful British student, a daughter of a diplomat. I always tried to sit next to her. She knew that I liked her and wanted me to be next to her.

My school years were a thrilling experience. The nuns at Saint Joseph School were excellent. They taught me to love learning and to study many subjects and languages, especially French, Latin, and Catechism. I was assigned to Sister Asunta, who became one of my favorite teachers. She was short and young, about thirty years old, and full of energy. Because it was a French school, she concentrated mostly on the history and geography of France. As my education progressed, I came to know a lot about France—and very little about Palestine— and spoke French more than any other language. *"Vive la liberté!"* was my favorite saying. She frequently complimented me as a good student and recognized my desire to learn everything she taught me. I began to speak with a French accent. My friends had fun with the way I rolled my Rs and laughed even more when I spoke and sounded the same in Hebrew.

The nuns lived in a convent adjacent to the school and church where they worshipped each morning at six o'clock. One day Sister Asunta asked me to become an altar boy to assist the priest at mass each day. It was difficult to recruit boys to commit themselves to the early morning since it was two hours before school started. She promised to tutor me privately for one half hour every day before school and said if I committed myself for one full year, she would pray for me that "God will reward me and will not allow me to fail in securing my place in Heaven." Totally convinced, I grabbed this "made-in-Heaven" offer and served faithfully, not only for one but for the next three years. In fact, Sister Asunta was not only my teacher, she was my friend. I confided in her and told her my secrets, and she told me some of hers. The nuns always covered their heads, but I saw her beautiful blond hair one day when she didn't notice that it was sticking out from her head covering. She knew that I had an innocent crush on her, and I like to think that she liked me, too.

During those days it was considered a privilege to attend school, so the nuns were authoritarian, with strict discipline. I remember one afternoon after lunch we were playing in the hallways because it was raining outside. We were chasing the girls, pretending we were fencing, using our arms to poke them on their breasts. Suddenly, we heard sharp clapping from Mother Superior, a sign to immediately stand at attention, to which we obediently complied. We trembled as we watched her red face. Then she signaled my friend to come forward and slapped him in front of the whole school. The echo of the slap was so loud and painful that we all felt it. This game was, of course, never repeated.

On a more harmonious occasion, a beautiful spring day in 1951, two nuns took our class on a field trip to the charming village of 'Ein Karim to explore our talents at water painting. This village was located in the mountains seven kilometers west of Jerusalem. The homes were spacious and beautifully built from limestone rock. Living up to its name, 'Ein Karim ("generous spring water") was the main source of irrigation for the olive orchards in the valley to its north. Based on archaeological evidence and history, the village is identified as the birthplace of John the Baptist, and it is believed that Christ and the Virgin Mary visited there many times.

Prior to 1948 'Ein Karim was the largest village in the district of Jerusalem. It was for a thousand years a model of Christians and Muslims living peacefully together. There were several churches and monasteries, of which the Church of John the Baptist was the most prominent. In addition, there was the fascinating mosque of caliph 'Omar Ibn al-Khattab with its majestic minaret. Fortunately, 'Ein Karim's churches, mosques, and homes were not destroyed by Zionists during the ethnic cleansing of Palestine.

Even though the field trip was exciting and educational, my first experience at painting scenery was not promising. However, my brother Daoud displayed a unique artistic gift and to this day continues to enjoy painting.

During our lunch break, Sister Asunta was eating tabbouleh ("supreme salad") made from an assortment of finely chopped vegetables and cracked wheat. We were astonished. We glanced at her in admiration, asking why she was eating this rabbit food. She responded, "Tabbouleh is one of the healthiest meals God ever invented for picnics." She proceeded to explain how this famous dish became a legend. Many years ago, possibly in 'Ein Karim, a group of nuns planned a picnic in the mountains but could not agree on what food to take with them. They decided that each nun would bring a surprise vegetable to share with the group. As they sat together to prepare the meal, each contributed one of the following ingredients: burghul, fresh parsley and mint, green onions, tomatoes, dried onions, cinnamon, salt and pepper, fresh lemon, and olive oil. They diced everything very fine in a big bowl and tossed it carefully for a good mix. When it was time to eat, they discovered that no one had brought any utensils, so one nun suggested that they eat the salad with their hands using the tender grape leaves and romaine lettuce she had picked from the monastery garden. As was customary in biblical times, they all ate with their right hand using the first three fingers, symbolizing the trinity of the Father, the Son, and the Holy Spirit. From then on, tabbouleh became popular as a supreme salad dish and a tradition throughout the Middle East.

After a few years at Saint Joseph, I grew too old for the girls' school, so I was transferred to Terra Sancta College for older boys. At the age of twelve, I was already able to converse in four languages. I spoke Arabic at home and with my friends, French at school with the teachers, Hebrew with the new Jewish colonial occupiers, and English with the British and American newcomers. I felt that speaking several languages gave me an advantage and the confidence to communicate with more people than most of my friends. Sometimes these languages were useful in expressing clichés or obscene words when defending myself during arguments.

Terra Sancta College (taken between 1920 and 1932)

Unlike Saint Joseph School, which was run by French nuns, Terra Sancta College was administered by Italian Franciscan priests. It was more suitable for boys, and I found it easier to make friends, which contributed to an even more joyous experience. We studied Arabic and English, and more advanced subjects like biology, math, and history. The priests were more authoritarian than the nuns, and it was customary at that time to punish the boys for bad behavior by hitting them with a ruler on the palms of their hands and on their derrière. It was foolish to tell our parents about this, because our parents would not only support the priest but tell them to punish us more the next time. Fortunately, I continued to be an altar boy on Sundays. Early those mornings, Fahima bathed me, ironed my best clothes, and dressed me for church. Terra Sancta in turn kept me out of trouble and on good terms with the priests.

Father Terrence was a dynamic priest and friendly to Palestinians. He taught me to ring the church bells on Sundays before mass. I jumped to pull the rope down to start the bells ringing and continued jumping and pulling continuously for about five minutes. Later I lit the candles, wore a robe, and was honored to read the scripture in Arabic, which made me very nervous in front of my family, friends, and the congregation. On holidays I assisted Father Terrence in lighting small coals to burn the frankincense gum resin during mass, which gave a distinct, sacred odor that stayed with me throughout the day. Sometimes after mass he discreetly let me taste the red wine and even gave me some pocket money from the offering basket in appreciation.

After our lunch break in school we often played soccer in the schoolyard, six or eight players on each team. Father Thomas frequently loved to join us in our game; he was a young and friendly priest. He would take his cap off and could run faster than most of us in his long brown robe. He played as aggressively as any of us, screaming, pushing, and calling fouls to stop the play. Sometimes when he was tired he would hide the ball between his feet under the robe. His team seemed always to win.

My high school graduation picture from the Terra Sancta school. (1958)

Since I had a close rapport with Father Thomas, my friend George, who was insecure about his height and longed to be taller, pressed me to go with him for a consultation. George asked Father Thomas, "How can I become tall as Ya'coub?" Father Thomas, puzzled by his question and not having a scientific medical answer, replied, "Each morning before school, stand facing against a wall. Stand on your toes with both your arms up, then stretch, stretch, stretch, altering one arm at a time for five minutes, every day. This will help you become taller." Poor George! Even though he took the Father's advice faithfully, when he finished high school he was still short, about five feet, while I sprouted to six feet and became the tallest person in my family.

More realistically, Father Terrence organized a new social recreation center for boys after school that was named the Terra Sancta Club. Initially, it was for the older students; my older brother Daoud and his very good friends Rizek and John were the founders. It was a place where boys could hang out, socialize, learn to dance, or play darts, backgammon, and cards, particularly Whist, a simplified bridge game. On Friday evenings and holidays the boys would decorate the club and invite their sisters, relatives, and friends. Of course, Father

89

Terrence was always there as chaperone. Dancing was very popular, especially the tango, samba, paso doble, and cha-cha. My brother Daoud teamed with my sister Fahima. They became an excellent dance couple since they practiced regularly at home, and Fahima sewed her own beautiful twirling dress. They were the hit of the club.

The club elected officers democratically, and it became the most popular place for Palestinians boys in West Jerusalem. As the boys grew older and moved on, the younger boys took over and followed in their footsteps. When my time came I became very active socially, learning to dance and play cards, all the while making new friends.

In the evenings when the club closed, we often walked along King David Street on the way home. One of my friends, Maurice Kattan, used to envy my athletic abilities. He liked to argue about how fast he could run and insisted he wanted to challenge me in a race in the middle of this famous street. Maurice was shorter and heavy, very unfit physically. I was not interested in racing him, but my other four friends wanted to settle it once for all. He proposed we run for one kilometer between the two light poles. I agreed but countered instead with "two kilometers, to the pole and back." The other friends appointed themselves starters and umpires. On the count of three we took off like rockets, running neck-and-neck for the first kilometer. After we made the turn, I got my second wind and accelerated, leaving him behind halfway into the second kilometer. Maurice finally conceded victory to me.

On another night, on the same street, we saw two policemen frantically chasing a young man down the crowded street. One of my friends shrewdly shouted loudly in Hebrew, "*A'ravi, A'ravi* [Arab, Arab] catch him, catch him!" Soon a mob joined the chase in pursuit. They caught and began to beat him, only to find out he was, in fact, Jewish!

9

MY REFUGE AT THE
JERUSALEM YMCA

The Terra Sancta school was near our home and within walking distance to the Jerusalem Young Men's Christian Association (YMCA). One afternoon after school, I walked to the Y to play in its beautiful outdoor garden. While I was sitting at the edge of a fish pond with my feet in the water, three older boys deliberately pushed me into the water. Fortunately I was saved from drowning by a physical education instructor who happened to see me struggling. He took me inside to the locker room to dry. Then he convinced me to join the Y for swimming classes. His name was Zeev Loewendal. I later learned that Zeev was the Y's physical education director. He became a good friend and mentor to me, and so began my long, fruitful association with this excellent organization. It not only got me off the streets but it gave me protection and introduced me to a wide range of productive activities.

The YMCA building (taken between 1934 and 1939)

The Y, now known as the Jerusalem International YMCA, was built in 1933 west of the Old City and is still considered one of the most beautiful YMCAs in the world. Its magnificent tower, named the Jesus Tower, stands across from the fabulous King David Hotel and is an architectural masterpiece. From the top of the 165-ft-high tower one can see a panoramic view of the entire city. Sketched maps engraved on the rails explain Jerusalem's historical landmarks. On a clear day one can see very far, sometimes as far as the shimmering waters of the Dead Sea, about thirty-nine kilometers east of Jerusalem, and the lowest point on the earth's surface.

To this day the building is decorated throughout with marvelous tiles engraved with biblical sayings. Inside the lobby, the walls and ceilings are covered with fascinating secular paintings. In the center, below the tower, is a three-story hotel for guests and dignitaries. The structure is balanced by two domes: on one side is the auditorium dome for music concerts, live shows, and cultural events; on the other side is a second dome, which houses the Physical Education Department. The facility also features a gymnasium, indoor swimming pool, squash courts, fitness center, locker rooms, outdoor tennis courts, and a track-and-field and soccer stadium in the back.

The Y was built as a monument to ecumenism. Its architectural décor, which embodies symbols of the three monotheistic religions, was designed as an attempt to create better understanding, harmony, and tolerance among all of Palestine's inhabitants. The Y was a multireligious center that included Christian, Muslim, and Jewish members, and that prided itself in working on interracial, interfaith, and peace-seeking activities, without distinction of creed, with all peoples. In 1947, and during the war in 1948, the Y housed the International Red Cross for refugee aid and became the center and headquarters of the United Nations Special Committee on Palestine under the first UN mediator, Count Bernadotte.[13]

After Zeev rescued me, I joined the Y, whose red triangle symbol stands for the human being as a whole through the unity of body, mind, and spirit. At the beginning, I saw the Y as a means to escape from my daily hardship. Instead it opened up an entire world for me. I found refuge and a sacred, personal space. Every day after school I went directly to the Y rather than going to the crowded and depressed flat in the zone where we were living on top of each other—five boys, three girls, my mother and father. I became heavily engaged in active sports, which kept my mind preoccupied and away from our daily hardship and struggle. In a real sense the Y became my home. I spent more hours there than at any other place, and it became the center of my life. I especially enjoyed having a hot shower each day, a luxury I did not have at our house in the zone. The soothing hot water running over my hair and down my back was a blessing, and I did not have to wrestle with my brothers for my turn squatting in the pitiful cold tub.

On my way home from the Y, I occasionally stopped at a watermelon stand owned by an old Palestinian farmer. He welcomed me and proudly offered me a slice or two of his sweet and juicy watermelon, or *battikha*. I enjoyed his company and meaningful conversations, and admired how he cherished and handled the fruit with care. He showed me the art of selecting the best watermelon by thumping, tapping, and carefully listening for a solid sound. "This watermelon is *ar'a*—bold, unripe, and not good to eat. This one is red, sweet,

Swimming for the Y swim team (1953)

juicy, and delicious." He then proceeded to explain the value and usefulness of the fruit. "The red sweet meat is nutritious and enjoyed by humans, the rind is consumed by donkeys and other animals, and the *bizer*, or seeds, are dried and then roasted for snacks. In a watermelon, nothing is wasted."

My attachment to the Y as a young child influenced my way of life not only with regard to sports, social, and recreation activities but also in terms of work. I started working as a lifeguard there and later taught

94

*My older sister Fadwa and I standing in front
of our apartment building in the Zone. (1958)*

swimming classes and served as a summer camp counselor. In one way or another, all my brothers and sisters had some connection with the Y. Mihran was involved in fitness, Daoud in tennis, Suleiman in weightlifting, and Zakaria in soccer. My sisters participated in dancing and social programs. There was always something for everyone.

I was physically fit, coordinated, well-built, and very competitive, and excelled in several sports at the same time. My competitiveness started when I was a child playing games, but as I became more athletic, taller, and stronger, I excelled in several sports. At times it was very difficult for me to coordinate my training because several coaches wanted me to practice on their teams—swimming, basketball, tennis, racquetball, or soccer. In high school I was on both the swimming and basketball teams at the same time. One of my

The YMCA swimming pool (taken between 1934 and 1939)

basketball teammates, David Kaminski, later became a big star and one of the best players in the country.

Swimming was a big sport at the Y since it had the only indoor pool in the country and trained one of the best teams. Between the ages of ten and sixteen, I became one of the best swimmers on the team, especially in the backstroke style. In 1955 I won the one hundred meter backstroke at the National Indoor Swimming Championship in Jerusalem, breaking the national record. During the same period, I won many other swimming meets in Jerusalem and around the country. I was slim, with distinct features, and developed a lean, toned body, which enabled me to glide smoothly through the water. I was in such excellent shape because I practiced twice daily, once in the early morning before school and again in the evening.

I swam hundreds of laps every day to become a successful athlete and to improve my persistence, flexibility, posture, and cardiovascular conditioning.

With my swimming skills and endurance, I also competed for three consecutive years in the *Tslihat Ha Kinneret*, or Lake Crossing Competition, swimming successfully across the width of *Buhairet Tabariya*, the Sea of Galilee. The distances were four kilometers (2.5 miles) the first year, five kilometers (3 miles) the second, and six kilometers (4 miles) the third. During this annual event I practiced and lived at the nearby kibbutz and was the only Palestinian participating out of hundreds of swimmers. Since the lake is formed from rivers and springs that run into and through it, there was always a rapid current flowing across the water that made swimming more challenging.

On my third crossing it was a very windy day, cold, and the water was rough. I was constantly struggling against the waves, and it seemed like I was swimming directly against the current. I swam mostly the freestyle

National indoor 100-meter backstroke winner and three-time participant and record holder in distance swimming competition across the Sea of Galilee. (1958)

97

crawl and had to stay focused to avoid drifting off course. Some swimmers didn't finish and had to be pulled out of the water because of muscle cramps or exhaustion; they were not fit enough for such a strenuous competition. Concerned and hesitant after watching swimmer after swimmer quit, I paused for a moment around the middle of the course to look back at the starting point and noticed that the distance was much farther than I expected. I then looked forward to the shoreline; it seemed too far off and indefinite. For a minute I didn't know if I could make it. Yet, I thought to myself, I have to keep moving ahead and reach the shore, there was no going back. The challenge was compelling and my choice was clear: I had to persevere and struggle to the finish line. Fortunately, I not only finished but did so in record-setting time.

One important benefit of long-distance swimming was that it offered me valuable time to think and contemplate. I particularly thought about my family's misfortune in our beloved country. I was determined to swim harder and faster against the rough water as a way to relieve my anger. Swimming, moreover, gave me freedom and the opportunity to think about the wonderful things I hoped to obtain in life. I felt confident that I could achieve my dreams.

When I was sixteen I took a class at the Y to get certified in scuba diving. The highlight of the program was a two-day trip to the resort port city of Eilat on the Gulf of A'qaba on the sparkling, deep-blue Red Sea. It was the same location where the famous explorer Jacques Cousteau filmed many of his first underwater movies. We were four divers—the instructor, two Jewish boys, and myself. On our first day we dove in shallow water, about six to eight feet deep, and not far from shore. The water was cool and crisply clear with an abundance of sea life below the surface. We saw many lovely colorful fish—yellow, red, blue—in all sizes and shapes. Some were weaving in synchronized schools, while others were chasing one another. On the bottom, we saw crabs and lobsters creeping among rocks and seashells. For a while I pretended I was swimming like a fish, or perhaps playing like a dolphin.

On the second day, the instructor took us farther away from the shore to deeper waters, between ten and twelve feet. The instructor's rule was to always use a "buddy system," two divers together, always staying next to each other. Deep down we swam next to a ridge that dropped off. Suddenly we encountered a rapid underwater current pulling us deeper, over the ridge. We tried to fight our way back, struggling and swimming harder, but it kept pulling us farther down. The instructor signaled to us to swim immediately to the surface. Exhausted, two of us made it the top, but the third diver had to be rescued by the instructor after a long battle with the current. It had been a close call, we later learned.

One of my best friends on our swim team was Daniel, a handsome Jewish boy with blond features, in contrast to my dark hair and olive skin, but with my same height and similar build. He was happy and easygoing, which made for a good friendship between us. We practiced swimming daily, ate and sat together on the bus during travel to swim meets, and competed vigorously against each other. We hoped to stay friends for life. When he became eighteen years old in 1957, he was drafted into the Israeli Air Force.[14] About a year later I learned that Daniel had lost his left leg after stepping on a mine and was recuperating at home. I tried repeatedly to see him, but he refused to meet me. I did not understand why we could not remain friends. I wondered, was it his new physical handicap? Sadly, I realized that maybe it was simply that he now only considered me as a Palestinian and perhaps even an enemy. The conflict, not his disability, had destroyed our friendship.

Throughout high school I had several duties at the Y, and because of my aquatic skills, I also worked as a life guard and swimming instructor at other luxury hotels in the city. At one of the major hotels I met Paul Newman, his wife Joanne Woodward, Eva Marie Saint, Sal Mineo, and other actors during the filming of the movie *Exodus.* I also met Leon Uris, who wrote the famous novel on which the film was based. One afternoon at a pool party, I had to rescue one of their crew members who was drowning in the water because he had previously been drowning in alcohol. They were all impressed. They thanked me and included me in their social gatherings, and later invited me to watch the shooting of the movie. They told me I could have a minor part in the movie, since they were looking for many types of characters, an offer that I politely declined since I had no desire to be associated with such a propaganda-like film.

In 1959, when I was eighteen, Zeev offered to send me for teacher training at the Wingate Sports Institute in Netanya on the Mediterranean coast. Wingate was the prime sports education school in the country. When I completed their training and certification, I was hired as the assistant physical education director of the Jerusalem YMCA. My responsibilities included teaching swimming, fitness, and basketball to youth classes and assisting the director in the administration of the department. I was very happy with my work and became well-accepted among the staff. Most full-time employees at the Y were Christian and Muslim Palestinians, except Zeev, who was Jewish and who became my good friend and supporter.

On my rare vacations, I drove with my friends to the Sea of Galilee to the peaceful retreat center of the Y's Peniel House. This was among the most pleasant memories of my youth. The property, at the time one of the most beautiful places on the sea, was bequeathed in the 1920s by Archibald Harte, general secretary of the Jerusalem International YMCA. Each morning I woke up at dawn for a dip in the fresh, spring-fed pool. During the day we hiked and explored around the volcanic rocks. There was an abundance of small and medium-sized fish that we had fun catching, especially Saint Peter's fish. Once in a while we camped in the garden next to the lake at night under the date trees. We made a small campfire to barbecue the fish we caught earlier that day. One of my favorite places at Peniel was sitting on the veranda that overlooked the beautiful lake. In the morning I could watch the sun rise over the calm water, and in the evening watch the moon glimmer over the silver and tranquil water. There I meditated and valued my solitude and peace of mind.

Occasionally we drove all the way down the south side of the lake to where it narrows and becomes the River Jordan. We enjoyed swimming in the warm water, even skinny dipping at times. Once in a while we witnessed Christian pilgrims praying in unison and being baptized not too far down the stream, where Jesus Christ was believed to have been baptized. The pilgrims walked in Jesus's footsteps and filled glass bottles with blessed "holy water" from the river to take back home.

During the summer, I sometimes traveled with the adult couples on Saturday's bus trips to the Mediterranean beaches to assist the life guards. As the bus was approaching Bat Yam near Tel Aviv, I remember how refreshing it was to smell the salt water breeze, and a few minutes later to be in sight of the vast, bright blue sea. It was refreshing to spend all day on the white sandy beaches, to get a good suntan, and watch all the beautiful girls in their skimpy bikinis. I could not understand why the Israelis were on the one hand projecting themselves to the world as a devout religious state, and on the other hand, instead of attending synagogue on the Sabbath, indulging in French Riviera-esque, nearly nude beaches. The beach scene didn't offend me, though. On the contrary, I enjoyed the atmosphere thoroughly.

One day, I met an American priest named Father Henry Fehrenbacher who was traveling through the Holy Land. He had used up all of his cash and travelers checks and knew no one in Jerusalem, so no one would cash his personal checks. I helped him get his checks cashed so he could take a plane to Greece.

In addition to visiting the holy sites in the city, Father Henry wanted to see the countryside where Jesus walked with his disciples. So I drove him on my Vespa to a mountain about fifteen minutes from the Y. We enjoyed hiking and took several pictures of the beautiful scenery and landscape. One surprise was an encounter with a young Palestinian shepherd tending his flock. Father Henry was excited and began to communicate in English with the shepherd who could not understand a word. I translated.

"What is your name?" he asked. "Mustafa," he gently replied. "Where do you live?" "There, over the mountain," he pointed, "in that village of Abu Ghosh." "Do you go to school?" "No." "What do you think about the future and Israel?" "You mean the Jews?" "Yes." "They should leave us alone and get out of our land." "Where should they go?" "Back to where they came from." "Can't you live with the Jews?" "Yes, I can live with them, but the new fanatics want to grab our land, take our freedom, and destroy our life."

Henry was struck by the shepherd's sincerity. He was a man who loved his homeland and understood his political and human rights. Through my chance acquaintance with Father Henry, I found new friendships that extended to America. Years later, when I came to the United States, I wound up staying with one of his students.

In addition to my duties at the Y, I instructed various sports to hundreds of kids. I also coached a youth basketball team, which became one of the best teams in the Jerusalem junior league—we were the team to beat. The players were Christian, Muslim, and Jewish kids, who became good friends and later my best fans. During my home games, they regularly tallied my basketball scores and brought me newspaper clippings to analyze each game at our next practice. They were especially enthusiastic about my high-scoring games, and I became their role model.

In September 1958 I reluctantly quit the swimming team to devote my energy to basketball. Within two years I became the youngest and one of the best players on the YMCA men's team, which played in Israel's *Ligah Alef* (League A). Because of my speed and agility, I was selected to play guard, now called point guard. I had an excellent dribble with both hands and a good drive to the basket. I passed the ball and assisted well, and had a great jump shot. At six feet I was considered tall and was able to dunk the ball at times. My brothers and several of my friends came regularly to see me play, particularly my home games. On one night I scored twenty-nine points in the second half to win the game. One of my enduring dreams was to become a basketball star, so I tried to emulate the famous American NBA player Oscar Robertson.

Fortunately, in the fall of 1958, I was introduced to and became a good friend of Jerry O'Dell. The son of a minister, Jerry was a tall, handsome, and free-spirited American who

*Above the competition as three-year top scorer
with the Jerusalem YMCA basketball team. (1960)*

was traveling throughout the Middle East on his bicycle and who ended up at the YMCA after running out of money. Because he was an excellent basketball and tennis player, he got a job at the Y, joined our team, and became one of my best teammates. We practiced together daily, and he introduced me to fundamental American basketball skills in ball handling, dribbling, and shooting. In a sense, he was a great influence who believed in my abilities. He told me that I would have been a better player in the US, with better training, opportunities, and a healthier lifestyle. I can honestly attribute my basketball success to Jerry, as he later coached our Y team.

For me basketball became a rite of passage and an important part of my life. I practiced day and night, and played well for the Y's team. My success attracted the attention of other coaches who wanted to recruit me to Israel's *Ligah Le'umit*, National Basketball League, in which Jerusalem had two rival teams, *Hapoel Yerushalaim* from the Labor Party and *Maccabi Yerushalaim* from the Herut Party. Both asked me to play for them. Even though I was not involved in politics and did not care for either party, I felt better playing for *Hapoel*. I had mixed feelings and a difficult time deciding whether I should join a Jewish team, because on the one hand I was the only Palestinian player on the team and in the entire league, and on the other hand I wanted to improve my athletic talent as a player to prove how good I could be. I took basketball seriously because it provided me with security and hope, and earned me respect.

My decision to play with *Hapoel Yerushalaim* in the National League proved to be the right choice. I soon became a starter and one of the leading scorers on the team. More importantly, I was the first and the only non-Jewish basketball player in the league, and in the country. We traveled across the country playing against teams in Tel Aviv, Haifa, Kibbutzim, and other cities. I was ranked and became a basketball star featured weekly in the sports papers, and was nicknamed the "Jerusalem Tiger"—*Nimer* (from *Nammari*) meaning tiger in both Arabic and Hebrew. Ironically, as my name was Ya'coub in Arabic and Ya'cov in Hebrew, there wasn't enough difference between the two names to notice, so I was treated like any Israeli citizen. Soon after, I was selected to join the Israeli National Basketball Team. During the regular league that season, I was ranked among the top seven players in the country.

Recently, after many years, Jerry and I got reacquainted, corresponding and reminiscing about our earlier basketball days in Jerusalem. He wrote me,

> How could I forget that skinny little guy who used to spend hours in the Y gym with me, throwing me the ball so I could practice, hour after hour, my shooting . . . Imagine my shock when in 1961 I returned to Jerusalem to find that tall, handsome guy who could out-dribble, out-jump, outrun, outshoot, and out-think me on the court. Luckily for me (though not so lucky for him), we played on the same team!

Jerry also reminded me of his experience trying to get a player's license when he tried to play in Israel again.

> When I returned to Israel for the second time in 1961, the basketball authorities gave me a hard time because I didn't have a player's license. When Zeev called their office and pointed out that another American student had been given his license right away, the reply was, "Yes, but he's a Jew." Zeev called up the newspapers and had the whole affair put in the papers and there was a big uproar; the public supported me and I got my license. [†]

תורה החלה כאימוניה, בהדרכת המאמן ג'ורג' דוידסו

At practice (with ball) as a member of Israel's national team in basketball, with our American coach, George Davidson (center). (1964)

BORN IN JERUSALEM, BORN PALESTINIAN

Yediot Aharonot Sport *December 16, 1962*
A Portrait: When I Am Sick, It Goes Well for Me

The hero of the game between Hapo'el Yerushala'yim and Hapo'el Haifa was not necessarily Yitzchak Noyman, who shot the victory basket, but 22-year-old player, Jacob Nammar. While sick with a cold and a hoarse voice, making him barely audible, Jacob spoke about his feelings following the sensational victory of his team, Hapo'el Yerushalayim,

How do you feel after such a victory in which you personally had a respectable part?
Unrelated to this game, I will tell you that I have been sick for the past few days and my finger is sprained. I walked onto the court with a fever, and my finger was hurting. Interestingly, when I am sick things go well for me. It happened twice when I played in the YMCA line-up in Ligah Alef.
You had a weak start, and you improved only in the second half. What happened?
At the beginning, I didn't want to play at all. The coach asked me to get on the court. I did. I had a strange feeling. The fever affected me. As the game progressed I was dazzled by it and completely forgot about my sickness.
What was the most tense moment in the game for you?
When the situation was 66:61 in our favor. I was taken out because of five fouls. At that moment it seemed that victory was slipping away from our hands.
Was that your best game?
(smiling) Not at all. Lately I have been in satisfactory shape, but I am still not satisfied with myself. I think that I am capable of much more.
In your opinion, will Hapo'el Yeruyshala'yim place better in the league at the end of the season?
It is still the beginning, but it seems to me that we are capable of winning all the home games. We have to improve our performances on the road, and then we will become one of the four elite teams.

Jacob Nammar has played basketball since his childhood, but he joined the team when he became a member of the YMCA. Nammar always felt capable of more, so when he asked to join a team in the elite league (Ligah le'Umit), the YMCA understood it and granted him a release. But in spite of his appearances in Hapo'el, Nammar did not end his relationship with the YMCA. Recently he was appointed to the position of Assistant Director for the Sports Department.
Nammar, who is 1.85 meters, is full of energy today and was happy to hear his teammates tell him, "If you would have been removed from the court earlier, we would have lost." (Sh. Berkowitz)

As a basketball star, I found myself to be quite an eligible bachelor. But as dating was limited for Palestinian women, I had more dates with foreign European tourists. During one basketball game, I broke my right wrist. The injury required X-rays, then a cast. At the hospital I met a lovely Jewish nurse who wrapped my wrist and treated my injury. She was friendly to the point that we exchanged phone numbers. I learned later that she saw me playing basketball and was eager to meet me. It was a coincidence meeting her at the hospital. We dated for over a year and became very serious and spent a lot of time together. She attended my home basketball games and loved to ride on my Vespa scooter to the Mediterranean beaches on weekends.

Her family had emigrated from Germany after World War II and spoke mostly Yiddish, and some broken Hebrew. Her mother was a sweet, loving woman and an outstanding nurse specializing in severe illnesses. She liked me even though she knew I was Palestinian. She invited me for dinners, made me feel welcome, and was happy to see me with her daughter. However, her stepfather, who spoke of surviving the Auschwitz concentration camp, was a bitter man with an ax to grind and nothing good to say about anything. Each time I saw him he would preach to me about the Holocaust, how much the world owed him, and how "Palestine was given to him by God," even though he himself was secular and knew I had nothing to do with the Holocaust. Yet, he unloaded his hatred on me. I explained to him, "The Jews have no right to take our homes and lands and must give them back to us." Unfortunately, he would not listen, and in time, my relationship with him became sour, which made my breakup with his daughter inevitable.

10

"YOU DO NOT BELONG HERE"

As much as my brothers and sisters tried to normalize their lives, their lives had already changed. Childhood had left them behind, and now they had a rather depressing existence. They spent most of their time simply waiting for a better life, a future. My sister Fahima had exceptional sewing talent and experience, so it was no surprise when she landed a job working at a sewing factory owned by a Jewish family that had emigrated from Morocco. At first they were good to her. But after she taught her skills to some new Jewish immigrants, her employers said, "This is Hebrew labor, for Jews only, not for Palestinians . . . We don't employ Arabs . . . We want you to leave the country. You do not belong here." In response Fahima argued, "Why leave? This is where I was born, and this is my land!" But the owners let her go.

Meanwhile, my brother Daoud worked at the King David Hotel as a bellboy. He later was promoted to telephone switchboard operator by the Swiss manager who recognized his multilingual talents. It was a good promotion even though he had to forgo the many tips he received from rich guests. He rapidly learned to operate the old switchboard for all incoming and outgoing calls. One advantage of this job was that it was much more relaxing than standing and carrying heavy luggage all day.

The hotel was always busy, as tourists and guests came from all over the world, especially from the United States. In the summer months it was popular with the rich Israelis who came to enjoy the coolness of the high-altitude, mountainous landscape of Jerusalem and escape the severe summer heat. Once a year an American Jewish textile millionaire visited Jerusalem and stayed at the hotel for a full month to conduct business. On one occasion, he donated a winter coat to every Israeli soldier to show his support for the military. He also once tipped Daoud with a one hundred dollar bill, which was a lot of money in those days.

Prime Minister David Ben-Gurion and his wife were important guests. They stayed at the hotel when they had meetings with foreign and local government dignitaries. On those occasions, the telephone became very busy, especially serving the prime minister and his wife. Ironically, the two were friendly to Daoud, not knowing that he was Palestinian, not Jewish. Daoud always felt awkward as a minority among Jews. He knew that the *mukhabarat* (Israeli security service) kept him under surveillance at all times. They always seemed to know everything about him—what he did, where he worked, where he went, and the friends he associated with. The *mukhabarat* had members of spy cells pretend to be his friends so they could get information about him.

Daoud was an outstanding tennis player. He recalled,

One spy jerk infiltrated our tennis team at the Y and envied my activities. He was jealous of my success, my work, the Jewish girl I dated, and my excellent tennis game. I suspect he must have known how Prime Minister Ben-Gurion trusted me with their personal telephone calls at the hotel.

Consequently, Daoud recounted,

I was summoned to the hotel manager's office and abruptly fired. What was the reason? The manager replied that even though he liked me as a person and an employee, he could not reveal the real reason. He said he had been ordered by some high government official to let me go, without revealing any names. I knew exactly who it was—the *mukhabarat* . . . [†]

The truth of the matter was that government spies and their superiors were envious of Daoud because he was intelligent, he stayed out of trouble, and minded his own business. Nevertheless, one afternoon two Shin Bet detectives picked him up and took him to the police station, accusing him of being a spy. The officers questioned him, "Who are you spying for and what have you told them?" The detectives kept him in prison for three days, along with convicted criminals. He recalled, "The place was like a dungeon out of the middle ages. Opposite my cell sat one of the worst Jewish criminals." Since they could find nothing against him, they finally released him to go back to the zone, our other military prison.

Rizek Abushaar, one of Daoud's best friends, who later became my colleague at the YMCA and a good friend, spoke of his ordeal being harassed by Shin Bet police officers. In the summer of 1957, after a long and hectic summer camp in Jerusalem, Rizek and his friend Anis traveled to the YMCA Peniel House at Lake Tiberius for a few days of rest and relaxation. They arrived at eleven o'clock in the morning, went swimming for about an hour, had lunch, took a siesta, and were suddenly awakened.

> At 2:00 pm a bang on the door woke me up. Two Jewish policemen came into the room and said, "You are under arrest." They frisked me and searched my suitcase and the bed. I asked to speak to Leslie Putnam, the general secretary of the Y in Jerusalem. They refused. . . For about half an hour they interrogated me asking superficial questions, while Anis stood by frightened and puzzled. Then, I was escorted to their car and taken to the Tiberius Police station and placed in a single cell.

After about an hour Rizek yelled to see their captain. The captain said, "I don't know the reason they picked you up, and I will send someone to take you to Jerusalem." Rizek spent two nights in the cell without any human contact, except when they brought him a tin plate with rotten sardines, which he refused to eat. For three days he ate nothing and drank only water. On the third day, at 3:00 pm, two policemen came to unlock his cell. One of the policemen recognized Rizek and didn't handcuff him. They put Rizek in the police car and drove away. The corporal swore that he didn't know why Rizek was under arrest.

To Rizek's astonishment they were taking him to Gedera, a small town south of Ashkelon. It was already nine o'clock in the evening. They placed him in another prison cell with eight other men.

> There was no toilet, except a hole in the corner of the room which smelled like a sewer. They gave us some nasty food, not fitting for dogs . . . I complained to the captain by refusing to eat this. I would rather die. A few minutes later, they brought some thin dirty mats for sleeping on the cement floor . . . Shortly after, the lights were turned off.

Later that same evening, a young Bedouin man, perhaps seventeen years old, was carried to the cell. He was bleeding profusely and crying. They placed him near Rizek. The young man explained to Rizek that he had been on a bus trip, missed his stop, and found himself in Ashkelon. He was interrogated by the police, beaten, and then brought to the prison. He was concerned and crying, not for himself but for his mother and father, who had lost his sister two weeks ago as a result of a snake bite. Early the next morning he thanked Rizek in a hushed voice because he didn't want anyone to know they were speaking in Arabic. Then policemen removed the man from the cell and took his mat away.

That morning, Rizek was taken to interrogation again.

Two men shone flashlights on me, put me in a bare, empty room . . . telling me that they intended to keep me here for seven years without trial because they thought I was a security risk. They falsely claimed that in 1956 I received a letter from someone in Zion Square in Jerusalem, and they wanted to know to whom I gave that letter. I explained to them that I had no recollection of any such encounter . . . that I never received such a letter and that I wanted a lie detector test. They began to laugh hysterically, telling me that as a prisoner, I cannot ask for anything. After three hours I was returned to the cell totally exhausted and dumbfounded. At 3:00 pm they came again and began a round of other ridiculous questions. "Who did I know?" "To whom did I give information?" Finally, after eight days and a lie detector test, they came and said I was free to go. I was instructed by the captain who released me that I must report at 8:00 am the next morning at the Russian Compound, a police detention center in Jerusalem. He said that Inspector David Hen will be waiting for me, and "If you talk about your ordeal to anyone, we will put you back in prison."

I had no idea where I was, so I took my stuff and went to a local barber who gave me a shave and shampoo. I was so hungry and went to a grocer and got a cold bottle of orange juice and a loaf of bread, which I devoured quickly. Then I took a bus from Tel Aviv heading to Jerusalem, packed with passengers. While standing for half an hour, I had severe stomach cramps which resulted in my fainting in the middle aisle of the bus between the feet of the other standing passengers. No one gave me a seat. I thought I was dying. Miraculously, I was awakened, wondering where I was, but thanking God when I saw that I was now back in Jerusalem. I was tired and must have lost six kilos and felt as though I had risen from the dead. [†]

For eight days Rizek's family, friends, and colleagues at the Y were in agony not knowing anything of his whereabouts. They even contacted the American Consulate to search for him, but without any results. It was only on the last day that they were advised that he had been detained in prison and was now released. When he finally reached home, Rizek was welcomed with open arms by his family and a large group of friends. "When I saw my family and the crowd, I broke down and wept like a baby."

Years earlier, Rizek and his family had sought refuge for months at the Rosary Sisters' convent, hiding while the Hogan militias came day or night to search the convent.

Another time, my brother Suleiman and his friend Pendy, who both loved to play in the garden of a nearby Armenian Church where we sometimes prayed, climbed the mulberry tree to eat the fruits and pick fresh leaves to feed their rabbits. The administrator of the church, an Armenian woman, did not like them to play there and always chased them away from the garden. One day she contacted the Israeli police, accusing Suleiman and Pendy of stealing the church's golden chalice and two expensive chandeliers that had been taken previously by unknown thieves. They both denied the accusation.

Nevertheless, the officers handcuffed and took both of them to the police station.

Baba and Mama were outraged. They protested and argued with the officers, demanding their immediate release. While they were being held in the prison for twelve hours, the same thieves came back to the church and stole some beautiful antique wooden pews. The police officers were compelled to release Suleiman and Pendy to go home. We heard that these pews were later seen at a nearby synagogue.

———

At this time my basketball game was at its peak, and I was on the threshold of a career. I practiced hard, was on top of my game, and was assured to make the national team. Unexpectedly, one day I was abruptly dropped from practice without explanation or justification. I was dumbfounded and shocked. Two weeks later I was taken off the national team. The American coach of Israel's national basketball team, George Davidson, who thought I was an excellent player and who sympathized with me, reluctantly told me that since the team was funded by Jewish Americans, it was unacceptable for a Palestinian to represent Israel in the upcoming Olympic Games. Instead, they recruited some American Jewish players.

I felt betrayed. The promise of basketball as an opportnity had evaporated. During my regular basketball games with the *Hapoel* team, people had started to speak to me in a different way. I was verbally abused in front of my fans by other players, and also by the referees. I felt terrible and humiliated. I heard the fans booing me. They called me "goy," a term for a non-Jew, and made other offensive remarks. "You don't represent Israel! Go home!" "You don't belong in this country!"

117

I resented the racist implication that I was somehow a "goy," even though I knew that to them I was just a Palestinian. Predictably, I began to be fouled out consistently, sometimes in the first half. This reminded me of an Arabic proverb: *"Darabani wa baka, sabakani wa ishtaka"*— "He hit me and started crying. Then, he ran ahead of me to tell the teacher I hit him." The team's business manager, David Krauz, our coach, and my teammates all sympathized with me and were respectful. They felt sorry and asked me to ignore these "despicable Jewish fanatics," as they called them. Unfortunately, the racial taunting became overwhelming and started to take a toll on me. I could not continue to play basketball in a country in which I was hated because of my race and religion, especially in my own city and on my own land.

(photograph omitted)

Yediot Aharonot Sport
October 12, 1963

Basketball Star Nammar

David Krauss, manger of Hapoel Yerushalayim returned to Jerusalem happy about our win in Holon. But was angry at the referee Nisim Kaoli: "Ya'acov Nammar had a technical foul, but when he went to shake hands with Danny Erez, the referees said—don't shake his hand, he did it intentionally! How can a referee say such a thing?"

"I was playing great and we were winning the game. The referee knew I was a Palestinian, could not accept it, and did everything to get me out of the game. He called false fouls, a technical, and discriminated against me using dirty language. Fortunately, he was finally caught by our manager!"

The discrimination I felt on the basketball team was the final straw. It was then that I made up my mind to leave my beloved al-Quds behind and pursue higher education, as Mama had encouraged me. She understood my pain more than anyone else. Sometimes it is not the easiest thing to do, she would say, but it is the right thing. My life had to change. I was not ready to surrender.

Yediot Aharonot Sport
November 28, 1963

"Israeli basketball is going to lose a promising talent next month. Ya'acov Nammar (in picture), a Hapoel Yerushalaim 'star' that hid behind the walls of the YMCA, where he is employed in the sports department, will leave Israel for four years.

Nammar, 22 years old, an Armenian Catholic from Jerusalem, will travel to the United States to study in Physical Education in Minneapolis. Because of his efforts the team won the last four games in the Championship League, so his teammates are trying to convince him to stay or delay his plans. But Nammar insisted that for family reasons he is leaning towards accepting the proposal to study in the United States."

119

11

MY FATHER, OUR ROCK

When I remember Baba, I always think of him as a positive and understanding man who made every effort to include me in his life. To say I looked up to him was an understatement. I viewed Baba as a strong man, a "rock," who was also gentle and loving. I admired and respected him particularly during these difficult times. To keep himself busy, he spent many hours working in his garden. He loved to grow a rich variety of vegetables and herbs such as tomatoes, lettuce, radishes, onions, artichokes, parsley, mint, and oregano. He also planted flowers like jasmine, which he strategically placed on both sides of the entrance of the garden to give off a fresh, beautiful aroma when visitors might pass through and enter our home.

Every evening Baba enjoyed sitting outside on the veranda, either sipping fresh coffee brewed specially by Wedad or drinking a glass of *arak,* licorice liqueur, before supper. On Saturday evenings he occasionally enjoyed a smoke of his *argileh*, water pipe, prepared by Fahima. On holidays Fahima would surprise him by decorating his *argileh* with a hand-made jasmine flower wreath from his garden.

Since Baba was skillful and hard working, with a lot of experience in cars and buses, he got a job working as a car mechanic at the downtown local Ford dealership. But after several months he was fired when the management hired new Jewish immigrants. He then drove the bus for our Saint Joseph School as a volunteer. Finally, because he spoke Turkish, he became a chauffeur for the Turkish Consulate in Jerusalem.

One night after a party at the consulate, all of a sudden he became very sick and could not work. We could see and feel his growing frustration at his inability to find work to provide for his family—it was a burden and a strain on his life. His shoulders became stooped and he began to lose weight, along with his self-esteem. His health was deteriorating rapidly. To pass the time, he taught me how to fix and maintain my Vespa scooter.

Baba didn't have any money to spend on himself, so one day Mama asked me if I would buy him a pack of cigarettes and a bottle of *arak* to cheer him up. Even though I knew that cigarettes were not good for him, I obliged, knowing it would make him feel better. Later that afternoon I saw Baba and Mama sitting on the veranda, smoking, drinking, and laughing together. It gave me some satisfaction, even if only for a moment.

Over time he became weaker and sicker. I could see his health declining day by day and his eyes sadden as his life became more and more difficult under the Occupation. Not only Mama but Wedad, Zakaria, and I all assumed the responsibility of caring for him. It was apparent that he could no longer attend to his daily garden chores, so we took turns watering, weeding, and picking fresh flowers daily to brighten his and Mama's mood.

One evening while Baba was having a drink on the veranda he asked me to sit next to him. I sensed he was lonely and wanted only to have some company. But instead he surprised me by giving me his golden pocket watch with its delicate chain, his only valuable possession. I knew it meant a great deal to him since he always guarded it closely and did not allow anyone else to handle it. I looked in his eyes with admiration and for the first time I saw myself in him. I thanked him deeply and felt honored to accept this very personal and meaningful gift. That night I stayed up in bed wide awake, overwhelmed by my emotions. I spent hours staring at the watch, mystified at the arms ticking all around until it finally put me to sleep. It was my first watch, and I have protected it throughout my life.

Traditionally, every year around December 18th the YMCA held a party for its staff and their family members and friends to decorate the Christmas tree in the lobby and to celebrate the lighting of the Tower. The party always included food, music, and Christmas carols. That evening, however, amid the holiday cheer I felt a strange intuition that something was wrong, so I left abruptly on my Vespa. When I got home I was shocked to learn that Baba had been taken by ambulance to the Hadassah Hospital accompanied by my youngest brother Zakaria. At the hospital I learned that he had passed away in the emergency room. Zakaria was traumatized and angry. He shouted, "Baba was alive when I brought him here. I don't understand why he died!" It was shocking, forceful, and brought tears to my eyes. All I could say to my young brother was, "Baba is now in God's hands and He will take good care of him."

Baba's death took us by surprise and was a severe, severe blow. We did not know what to do. We asked the hospital to leave his body there for twenty-four hours to give us time to make funeral arrangements. Unfortunately, only Mama, Wedad, Zakaria, and I were around. Five of the mostly older children—Mihran, Fahima, Daoud, Suleiman, and Fadwa—had already emigrated.

Mama told me that Baba's wishes were to be buried at the Jerusalem Mamila Cemetery with his parents, grandparents, and family. The *ma'bara,* or graveyard, was located in West Jerusalem and considered historically significant as it dates back to the seventh century of the Ayyubid and Mamluk dynasties. Over seventy thousand of Salah El Din's warriors, who defeated the Crusaders in the Seige of Jerusalem in 1187, are buried there, along with other great leaders.[15]

We could not get a permit so it was impossible to bury Baba in the Mamila Cemetery. After a great deal of agonizing and soul searching, we finally buried Baba in the village of Beit Safafa, six kilometers southwest of Jerusalem. I had friends who lived there and who worked with me at the Y. They were very understanding and volunteered to help us with the *Janazah,* or funeral arrangements. It was a small Janazah on a cold winter afternoon. Only Mama, Wedad, Zakaria, and I were present from our family. For a moment I looked across the border fence hoping to see my brother Suleiman, but he was not there.

At the cemetery my friends helped dig the grave and participated in the funeral, which was considered an honor and came with the belief that one day one would be rewarded in heaven for doing so. As was customary, being the oldest son present, I had the honor to participate in the ritual to assist in the prayer, washing his body, and swaddling him with a white shroud to prepare him for burial. I prayed to God that he may rest in peace and his soul go into Heaven.

As Baba made his final journey, I grieved intensely and cried from a deep sense of pain. He died at the young age of sixty-one. As tears flowed down my cheeks, my last word to Baba before he was buried was that I would honor his memory, and I asked him for strength and guidance to carry the torch of our family legacy. Even though he had lost everything, he was a proud man and he had died with dignity.

My sister, Wedad, who was also with Baba during his last moments, remembered him in this way:

> One of the happiest times in my memories with Baba was in our garden. Since he was sick and couldn't garden anymore, I wanted to plant a Spanish fragrant violet and needed Baba to show me the way. As I was planting the flower in the dirt, I asked him if he was sure this would grow well, and he assured me to wait and watch for it in spring. Sadly, Baba passed away in December and didn't make it for the spring. However, when spring came, the violet flower was in great bloom which brought tears to my eyes with sweet memories of Baba's last words. [†]

Many years of stored tears rushed Wedad's cheeks as she recounted her past feelings.

I believe that my father, our rock, passed away from a broken heart. With his death, we lost the keystone of our family. His sudden death was painful to all of us, especially Mama who mourned for one whole year by wearing black and praying every day. She never remarried. Even though Mama suffered immensely, she was a survivor and subsequently devoted all her life to raising her children, finding strength in her faith.

For the first time in my life, with the loss of Baba, I felt a deep emptiness. I would never again see his penetrating dark eyes, or feel his unwavering compassion. Baba would not be there to guide us with his wisdom or to comfort or protect us. We became nearly hopeless after losing the center of our life, our stability, and safety.

12

EXODUS: ONE MOONLESS NIGHT

A few months before my father's death, my brothers Daoud and Suleiman accepted a good job opportunity. They both were hired as tool pushers by an American oil drilling company that had come to the region to conduct oil exploration in Israel. But Daoud and Suleiman were soon fired, even though the manager became a personal friend of our family. They were told that the oil exploration site was in the Negev Desert and off-limits to Palestinians. We thought perhaps that the government did not want them to know about the Dimona nuclear plant, which is located there in the desert. Subsequently, the company found no oil in Israel and decided to relocate to Jordan.

Suleiman, being a bit audacious, decided to follow the company by crossing the border illegally into Jordan through the village of Beit Safafa, where my father was buried. The 1949 Armistice Line, which became the border between Israel and Jordan, ran through the middle of the town, dividing the village with barbed wire. The fence also divided many families, which created hardship and resentment. But the villagers would openly communicate across the fence and sometimes exchange letters and gifts or witness the weddings of their relatives.

One night Suleiman daringly, and perhaps carelessly, jumped over the fence and managed to cross safely. On the other side he was met and apprehended by Jordanian authorities who accused him of being an informant and a spy for Israel, and put him in jail. After a month of interrogation some of our relatives arranged for his release, but he was placed under surveillance and forbidden to leave the country. Worse than that, Israel now considered him a fugitive and a counterspy, or double agent, for Jordan. He was forbidden ever to return to his family in Israel and was forced to remain in Jordan where he was able to live with our aunt. So Suleiman had become caught in the political turmoil between two warring countries: the Hashemite Kingdom of Jordan, whose ruler was paranoid about a suspected Communist plot to overthrow his kingdom, and the State of Israel, which was in the midst of trying to convince Western governments to legitimize its illegal creation on stolen Palestinian lands.

Suleiman's ordeal reminds me of the sad fate of our dog Laddie. One afternoon we were playing away from home close to the border with Jordan near the no man's land. While chasing a cat, Laddie strayed away and crossed the line. He was immediately shot by Israeli soldiers. This senseless killing hurt me deeply. We later discovered that this type of killing was routine policy—"shoot first and ask questions later." After becoming aware of this, we grew even more concerned about Suleiman and the dangers of crossing the border. We feared greatly for his life.

Following Suleiman's escape to Jordan, and with no stable employment opportunities in sight, one by one most of my other brothers and sisters started to emigrate. Initially, both Baba and Mama had been against splitting the family apart. At the same time they knew that there was no future for us in our homeland under Zionist control.

The first to leave was Fahima, who got married and moved to Texas in the US. She was followed by Mihran who enrolled in a college in Minneapolis, then Daoud who enrolled at North Dakota State University. Fadwa moved to Lausanne, Switzerland, for work opportunities and to further her education. After about a year she married and settled there.

As for the rest of the family—Mama, Wedad, Zakaria, and I—who remained in Jerusalem, life became progressively more intolerable. As the Israelis were getting stronger and the Palestinians weaker, our survival grew more difficult day by day as we struggled to make ends meet. We had to restructure our lives by combining our low wages to pay the bills. There was no extra money to spend on personal entertainment or luxury. The search for our future and dignity encompassed our livelihoods.

Six months later, Mama and Wedad became completely disenchanted with their lives in Israel, so they decided to leave together for the United States to join Mihran, Fahima, and Daoud. Zakaria, who was seventeen years old, stayed with me. I was twenty. Mama asked Wedad to stop in Rome to visit Vatican City on her way to America. Her dream was to one day meet the Pope for his blessing. Sadly, she was disappointed since the Pope was away at the time. From Italy they continued on to the United States.

Mama and Wedad arrived in St. Paul, Minnesota in the summer of 1962. However, after visiting her children for a few months, she became homesick and disappointed in America's fast way of life. She decided to return alone to Jerusalem, while Wedad remained to attend the University of Minnesota. Back in West Jerusalem, Mama became unhappy again and felt that there was nothing left for her in Israel. She said that it was difficult for her to stay in a discriminatory and racist society and that she wanted to move across the border to East Jerusalem so she could live and pray at the Holy Places. She was convinced that life would be better for her in the Old City, which was under the Jordanian control. She believed that the future would be more secure, particularly for my youngest brother, Zakaria, who was unsettled and discontent. Mama also wanted to be with my other brother Suleiman, his wife, and two kids, and to be closer to our aunt, cousins, and friends.

After Mama and Zakaria moved to East Jerusalem in the fall of 1963, I was left alone in West Jerusalem. I began to spend the majority of my time at the YMCA, opening the health and physical education department at six o'clock in the morning to teach swimming classes for students before school started. During the day I conducted adult fitness classes, and after school I ran physical education programs and coached youth basketball. Every evening I stayed late to close the department at 10:00 pm after our basketball team practice. But the hardship and long hours began to take a toll on me. My loneliness became such that it was necessary for management to give me a room at the Y to live in on the third floor. On the one hand I felt that I was an accomplished assistant physical education director and a basketball star living in the most beautiful YMCA in the world; and on the other hand, I was a lonely man, abandoned by my family. I began to question my future once more.

During my breaks from work and when I was depressed, I often found myself sitting alone at the back of the Y auditorium listening to the Israeli Symphony Orchestra practicing. I never understood why I loved classical music. I would spend hours at a time by myself, daydreaming. On one occasion I was disturbed by the janitors who asked me what satisfaction I was getting from listening to this "Zionist music." At that moment the orchestra was practicing the *Hatikva,* the national anthem of Israel. I answered, that with the exception of the anthem, the music was beautiful. I just hoped that the Israeli government could become as peaceful as this music. They shook their heads and thought I must be dreaming. They didn't believe this could happen.

Many times, I found myself alone praying to God, in Arabic. I have been inspired by many religions and my values have been enriched by the lives of peace seekers like Jesus, Mohammad, Gandhi, Martin Luther King, and others. But my own political philosophy was to be a global citizen, a person devoted to interfaith and interracial understanding, and who stands for human rights, justice, freedom, and peace for all people. For instance, basketball for me was much more than a game. I wanted to make a difference. I looked at basketball as a means to create harmony, a moderate way to bridge the gap between Christians, Jews, and Muslims and create a more peaceful existence. I wanted to cross racial borders in our community to open the doors and let the hatred and discrimination out. I still prayed and hoped for peace in Jerusalem.

I was never vengeful against Jews. I was against the racist policies directed toward us. The Jewish religion has many remarkable qualities, but few of them were reflected in Israel's militaristic society. I had several Jewish friends, especially in sports. I lived with them, ate their food, read their newspapers and books, and learned Hebrew. Ironically, because of the similarities between Hebrew and Arabic as Semitic languages, it was easy for me to learn Hebrew. In fact, I spoke Hebrew better than most of the new Israelis who were transplants from Russia, Eastern Europe, and America, and whose languages, accents, and customs were largely out of place and seemed not to belong in the Holy Land. On several occasions I was compelled to translate and help those Ashkenazis.

When I wanted to learn more about the Jewish tragedy, my Jewish girlfriend took me to visit the Hall of Remembrance at the Yad Vashem Holocaust Memorial in Jerusalem. We also took a trip to tour Masada, a Roman fortress in the desert southeast of Jerusalem, where it is believed that during the first century about one thousand ancient Hebrews committed mass suicide rather than being captured by the Roman soldiers. I felt it was important for me to witness and understand their horrific history. I tried hard to assimilate with my Jewish friends. My experiences in my teen years were amicable because not all of my Jewish friends supported Israel's policies; some opposed the government, particularly its policies towards Palestinian human rights. However, there seemed to be a sharp divide between those who strived for coexistence and those who strived for domination.

My Jewish friends were in a minority, as the majority supported the discrimination against Palestinian rights and defended racism at all costs—they simply refused to acknowledge the truth about their role in uprooting us. They behaved like a herd of sheep, grazing on our land and prospering as if they were born here and owned it legally, without any moral justification or feelings of guilt or remorse toward the Palestinians. My fundamental problem with the Jews was that they wanted to control all of Palestine and were not genuinely interested in a sincere dialogue to coexist and live together in peace. The unconditional support of Jews for Israel's behavior is described by Erskine Childers:

> We came and turned the native Arabs into tragic refugees. And still we have to slander and malign them, to besmirch their name. Instead of being deeply ashamed of what we did and trying to undo some of the evil we committed . . . we justify our terrible acts and even attempt to glorify them.[16]

As time wore on, it became increasingly difficult to understand why the Jews treated us so inhumanely. It is ironic that Jews, who were themselves victims, had become the oppressor who refused to recognize our right to exist. Israeli government officials and apologists refused to acknowledge any responsibility for the Nakba. By contrast, Zionists were quick to condemn as anti-Semitic anyone who questioned or denied the Jewish *Shoah*, the Holocaust.

Every year on May 15th I watched in dismay as Israelis publicly celebrated the creation of the State of Israel while we Palestinians were forced to quietly remember the dispossession of our own people as a direct result. They paraded their military force, singing and dancing in our streets. They glorified Jewish symbols, particularly the flag with the Star of David and the menorah, in the center of the city. At the same time, they prohibited us from identifying ourselves as Palestinians, as Arab minorities, no matter if we were Christian or Muslim. They made it a crime to mention the word Nakba or possess any Palestinian symbol, on a flag or t-shirt, or listen to any Palestinian patriotic poems and songs. How could I identify with such a state or sing Israel's national anthem when it glorifies only the "Jewish soul"?

I grew up as a minority amid constant threats and fear of the watchful eyes of the Shin Bet secret police. They seemed to have agents everywhere we went. It was like swimming in a sea full of sharks. We could not tell the good guys from the bad. They were disguised in military or police uniforms, or as male or female civilians. At one point or another, they spied on and interrogated almost each and every person in my family, and many of my friends. It became a continuous routine of Gestapo-like harassment, bullying, and intimidation.

I saw Palestine fragmented and destroyed as it drifted away from being a peaceful, productive, and prosperous country. What Israel eventually would do to the vital *Nahr al-Urdun*, the River Jordan, would become a tragic analogy for what has happened to the Palestinian people. Historically, the river's waters rise on Mount Hermon, nurtured by streams of the Hasbani River from the Shebaa Farms in Lebanon and the Banias River in the Golan Heights in Syria. The vital tributaries rapidly drop south to Lake Hula, then flow to *Buhairet Tabaraya*, or Lake Tiberius. After it runs through this beautiful fertile lake, it exits to form the basin of the River Jordan. The river then becomes the border between Palestine on the west—the West Bank—and the Kingdom of Jordan on the east. Then it continues to its final destination, the Dead Sea.

Like the plentiful olive trees planted in Palestine, the river was once fertile with abundant fresh, clean water shared by inhabitants of Lebanon, Syria, Jordan, and Palestine. Now, as it flows through Israel, most of the water is diverted to irrigate Israeli land, including the desert, depriving Palestinians of their life blood—their water—and causing ecological catastrophe and economic deprivation. What remains is a bed of muddied water trickling into the Dead Sea. An historic river is suffering a slow death, one drop at a time.

Like the River Jordan now, my personal life then was changing for the worse, coming to a slow and measly trickle and dead end. It had become abundantly clear to me that my days in Jerusalem were coming to an end. I had to pick myself up and move on. The possibility of a better future in my homeland had vanished. My childhood had proved challenging but energized with experiences that had strengthened my path to adulthood. Now I was alone and had to create my own destiny by making the most difficult decision of my young life. I was compelled to leave Jerusalem, to seek refuge.

My last experiences of Israel were sour. It was a state that didn't afford me a voice, economic independence, or a future. It had torn apart my home, my family, and my sense of a cohesive self, and had dispossessed not only me but my entire society. I could not live in a state that had been created by terror and illegal confiscation of my home, land, and personal freedom. I lost faith in such a state. What "starts crooked, remains crooked," says the Arabic proverb. Israel's so-called democracy lacked the vital elements that I learned as a child in my French school: liberty, equality, and fraternity. I believed that I and all Palestinians were entitled to and deserved these principles.

On my last day at the Y, September 1, 1964, I made the rounds to all my friends to express *Shukran Kathiran,* "many thanks"; in turn, they wished me *Allah Ma'ak,* "May God be with you." Then I climbed up to the top of the YMCA Tower for a final panoramic glimpse of the Old City, the symbol of the heart and soul of Jerusalem. I admired the blue skies and mountains surrounding the city. The gorgeous sunset accentuated the beauty of the landscape. As I looked out at East Jerusalem's familiar scenes, I could see the great Old City wall built by Suleiman the Magnificent in the sixteenth century, surrounded by old cemeteries and olive and pine trees. At the center of the skyline stood the golden Dome of the Rock and the towering Church of St. Mary Magdalene, further south the Russian Church at Jabal al-Tur, and the Dormition Church on Mount Zion, the place of the "falling asleep" of the Virgin Mary. I knew that these monuments represented something extraordinary—a place to worship my faith, to remain connected to my land, and to maintain my historical identity and a sense of pride. It was not the buildings or monuments that were most significant but rather what happened inside and around these places. As I gazed on the city, I reminded myself not to forget.

While I was meditating on top of the tower, I remembered what my father said to me before he died, "Enjoy your life; enjoy what you are doing." This wonderful thought brought me back briefly to childhood memories when I escaped to seek refuge in Battir, lost in both time and space. I thought back to being all alone in Battir, walking along the railway tracks, meeting the *fellaha*, riding on the donkey with her, trusting her, and being secure in her arms. The experience and adventure were important and stood out in my mind. I reminisced about playing in Haret al-Nammareh, the place I lived, growing up with my family's values, my traditional upbringing, the togetherness and simplicity of it all. I recalled living a way of life I couldn't find or live anymore. I was yearning to return to the place where I was born, where I belonged, a place where I wanted to live, the land where someday I hoped to die and be buried with my ancestors in the terra sancta, the Holy Land.

My own life in Jerusalem would end early the following morning. I was the last person from my family to leave my beloved Jerusalem and Palestine. I knew that I would always miss al-Quds. Our family's exodus brutally changed our lives forever. All I had was my attachment to our land and my childhood memories. As the poet Kahlil Gibran reminded me, "The most beautiful thing in life is that our souls remain hovering over the places where we once enjoyed ourselves."[17]

That dark, moonless, late-summer night, Jerusalem lay quiet and cool. The tranquility of the Holy City was broken by my footsteps as I headed home and by the murmur of the breeze as it drifted, whispering through the dark green leaves of the olive trees along the road. Once at home, I packed my traveling bag, my one-way airline ticket, my Israeli passport, and my one hundred fifty dollars in savings. Then I went to bed, hoping to get some sleep so as to wake up early the next morning in time to catch a scheduled flight to America. Tired as I was, sleep would not come. I remained wide awake all through the night, enveloped in thoughts and memories of my childhood, with twinges of hope and trepidation at the unforeseen future.

EPILOGUE

I am a man with a broken heart. I am from Jerusalem, my broken homeland, and Palestine makes me weep. Yet, I still have some memories to share and a story to tell. So I wish to add my own story to those of others who have lived through the ethnic cleansing of Palestine.

When I was seven years old, I became a victim, and survivor, of the Nakba. The more I remember, the more precious my memories become to me—memories of my family, of challenges and suffering, of open wounds, and of Israel's dispossession of the Palestinian people.

The dreams and memories of my childhood in Jerusalem and Haret al-Nammareh have always been with me. But more recently, as I began to look back and to reflect on my early years—between 1941 when I was born and 1964 when I left my homeland—I have felt a sense of urgency. I remember how we lost our home and land, and I see the result of Israel's domination today.

So I have written about our life and how our peaceable,

well-established family was uprooted and driven from our homeland. But my story is part of the expressions of a whole generation of Palestinians who lived through ethnic cleansing and exile, a process that began in 1948 and that has never stopped to this day.

I am growing older, my hair is turning salt-and-pepper. I am becoming more fatigued to witness before my eyes Israel's ongoing destruction of Palestinian society. I have sensed that it is time for me to bring to light realities that many around me have felt afraid to talk about.

While living in America I came to appreciate my uniqueness in being born and growing up in Jerusalem. I was fortunate to have lived and experienced childhood in Palestine, youth in Israel, and adulthood in America. During these transitions my name changed from Ya'coub to Ya'cov and finally to Jacob. I learned to understand and immerse myself in these three cultures.

In America I began a process of healing and self-liberation that brought me a renewed sense of hope. I learned to believe in democracy, to acquire knowledge, to work hard, to dedicate my life to ideals of freedom, equality, human rights, and the rule of law. I found most of my friends—and Americans in general—to be kind, generous, and compassionate people who were interested in justice, freedom, and democracy. America, after World War II, was seen as a beacon of freedom and light, the forefront of idealism, liberty, and human rights. Everyone wanted to be an American, including myself. I became patriotic and fell in love with America, my adopted country, as much as my country of origin. It offered me, my wife, and my three children prosperity, security, and purpose in life.

When I became a university student, I spoke to groups in

the community to help pay for my education. I became a non-violent peace and human rights activist. I joined peace organizations and wrote and spoke at every opportunity—radio, television, for groups promoting justice for the Palestinians—as a Palestinian Christian from Jerusalem.

Because of Israel's policies, most of my brothers and sisters have been reluctant to visit their homeland since they left about sixty years ago. I have made several trips to Palestine-Israel, and each time I became more outraged to see the conditions of Palestinians there. Israel has made it very difficult for Palestinians in the diaspora to visit their homeland, even with an American passport. The US Government is well aware of these violations but has done little to protect American citizens. What is most disturbing is that Israel refuses to honor US passports and deports American citizens of Palestinian origin, citizens who pay their taxes which, in turn, support Israel militarily, politically, and economically.

My brothers and sisters were apprehensive to tell their stories, some of which were too painful to cover in this book. They felt an enormous sense of frustration and trauma, or they could not recount dreadful events. I am grateful that they opened up to me. I have now told something of our story, even if it is not the whole story but a mere glimpse from childhood. If for no other reason, I want our children to be proud of our Palestinian heritage and roots. I want them to know that their parents, grandparents, and ancestors are originally Palestinians who have land in Jerusalem and an important history. We have a rich legacy and tradition, including valuable knowledge about our family.

It would be incomplete to finish my story without remembering Mama's last days in this world. Mama never remarried and was very lonely after Baba passed away in 1961.

In 1968, while I was a graduate student, Mama came to live with me and Nancy, my wife then, soon after the birth of Jacquetta, our first daughter. Since most of us children had already moved to North America, she was left alone in East Jerusalem. She decided to pack up her few belongings and buy a one-way airline ticket to the US. She was excited to meet my wife and to witness my daughter's baptism, which was conducted by my very good friend Father Clarence Thomson.

Once again in 1971 Mama was thrilled with the birth of our second daughter, Jeneen. She was very happy to live with us and loved our girls dearly. She was also very happy that all my brothers and sisters were now married with young families, exclaiming, "All I have left are my children." She taught us how to wrap the babies firmly with a blanket to keep them warm and secure at night. Before bedtime, she played with them, rocked them, and sang Armenian lullabies to put the girls to sleep. During the daytime, she played with the girls and insisted on cooking and helping with house chores. Mama loved to knit sweaters and slippers for her grandchildren. Even though she didn't speak English very well, to pass the time she watched television, especially "the soaps." Later she would critique them: "This good man . . . this bad woman . . . this man and woman no good together . . . These two people are beautiful together."

A special time for Mama was when she would wait for me each day to return from work so we could enjoy a drink together before dinner. We talked for hours, reminiscing about Baba, Jerusalem, Palestine. These were good times. Mama was a beautiful, petite lady who could not handle more than one drink. But she loved whiskey and red wine, and once in a while she had two or three, which made her high and tipsy. She would ask me to play some Arabic music, and she would put on all her jewelry, a little red lipstick, wrap a scarf around her hips, and start belly dancing. She would have my wife, little daughters, and I up and dancing all together. Often, when we were invited to friends' parties, she was the main attraction. She cooked her favorite Palestinian dishes and was even featured in the local newspaper. Everyone loved her.

Mama had endured the Armenian genocide, the Palestinian ethnic cleansing, a Zionist prison zone, poverty, dispossession of her home and land, and the death of her soul mate. But she never lost her love for life, or hope, or her faith in God. Each morning after she woke up she stood in front of the patio door and looked up to heaven, made the sign of the cross, and bowed her head to pray just as she did when she lived in Jerusalem.

She passed away suddenly from a heart attack in the summer of 1973 while visiting my brother Suleiman in Toronto. She had told me that when she died, her desire was to be buried next to Baba, in Jerusalem. Unfortunately, the Israeli authorities denied her wishes. Mama was survived by her eight children—five brothers and three sisters—and her twenty-five grandchildren and thirty great-grandchildren.

Mama left us with so many great memories. Recently my wife confided,

> I remember Mama with such fondness, admiration, and love. What a privilege to have had her in my life . . . She was kind, tolerant, and loving . . . I learned so much from her, loved her deeply, and admired how she never was about materialism, just lived each day and was grateful . . . She gave us so much in such a short time. [†]

"If, one day, a people desires to live, then fate will answer their call."

—Abu al-Qasim al-Shabi[18]

When the Tunisian poet Abu al-Qasim al-Shabi wrote this line in the early twentieth century, his country was under a brutal French colonial occupation and a popular national uprising movement for independence was underway. I remember first being introduced to his poem, "The Will of Life," when I was a student studying Arabic at the Terra Sancta school. It was then that I learned of the effect the poem had on the Tunisian masses in their struggle for freedom and self-determination. The uprising brought a new spirit (*ruh jedid*), which inspired me to hope and pray that Palestinians would soon take their fate into their own hands.

Now, years later, I have seen demonstrators marching once again in the streets of Tunisia against their oppressive ruler, chanting verses from al-Shabi's poem and demanding justice and equality in a civil society. The tragic self-immolation on December 17, 2010, of Mohammed Bouazizi, the vendor assaulted and humiliated in public by Tunisian police for trying to make a living selling fruit on the street, spread the fire of egalitarianism across Arab countries, from Tunisia to Egypt, Yemen, Libya, Bahrain, Syria, and beyond. Many of these countries, which also suffer from poverty, unemployment, and corruption, soon followed suit by taking to their streets and setting proverbial fire to entire corrupt and bureaucratic regimes. Perhaps the time has come when citizens of the Arab world can liberate themselves from dictators elected through deceit or appointed as puppet governments dominated by the West.

Even though Palestine has not been at peace for generations now, I believe and dream that one day we will have peace where all the children of Abraham—Christians, Muslims, and Jews—will live harmoniously once again in the Holy Land as equal citizens.

Perhaps it is time now to reclaim a history similar to my own youthful memories when the spirit of Palestine was that of a diverse, open society of freedom and equal rights for its entire people.

Jerusalemites have worked, worshipped, played, studied, and prospered together despite their turbulent history. Well before the British and Israeli occupations, they built water systems, new suburbs, hotels and inns, shopping areas, parks, museums, theaters, post offices, and telegraph facilities. They developed roads and railways connecting them to other cities. The city was a popular and vibrant multicultural community that was divided into religious neighborhoods but whose citizens worked and prospered together.

More importantly, Christian, Muslim, and Jewish natives lived in peace together. Jerusalemite society included many ethnic groups—Armenian, German, Greek, Italian, Russian, Ethiopian, and Assyrian representing Catholics, Orthodox Christians, Muslims, Jews (Sephardi and Mizrahi), Druze, and others. In many cases they intermarried and converted from one religion to another, learning to coexist as proud citizens of al-Quds. They and their children grew up going to schools and public facilities together. They communicated with each other in Arabic and identified as Palestinians, regardless of religious or cultural background.

I remember how each year, especially during holidays, Christians, Muslims, and Jews from all over the world made their pilgrimage and converged on "*al-ard al-muqadassa al mubaraka,* the blessed Holy Land and on the Old City of al-Quds. Devoted visitors navigated the narrow, shared alleys to worship in their respective holy shrines. When I was young, Jerusalemites prayed separately but then got together to conduct business, share a cup of coffee, celebrate, and console each other on sad occasions such as deaths and illnesses.

Christians, Muslims, and Jews came to Jerusalem from around the world because of its significance to their deeply rooted faith in their beliefs of the past, present, and future. I remember how faithful Christian pilgrims came from America and Europe during Easter and Christmas. They came to the Church of the Nativity in Bethlehem to pray at the place where it has been said Jesus Christ was born in a manger. They came to the Church of the Holy Sepulcher, the Church of the Resurrection—the traditional site of Jesus's burial. In the middle of the Church is a compass that Christians believe is the center of the world. Jointly administered by Catholics, Greek Orthodox, and Armenians, the key to the large gate to this church has been entrusted to a Muslim family for many centuries, a respected arrangement arrived at by the Christian sects to avoid conflict among them. Christians came to pray at Golgotha, the scene of the crucifixion, but also to visit Islamic or Jewish holy sites in reverence and awe.

Before 1948 Muslim pilgrims came from as far away as the Philippines, Pakistan, China, Turkey, Sudan, and Saudi Arabia. After they made their *hajj* to Mecca, they would visit our city, as it contains the third holiest site in Islam, after the mosques in Mecca and Medina. They worshipped standing and kneeling together, reciting the Holy Qur'an at the silver-domed al-Aqsa Mosque and at the Dome of the Rock (Haram al-Sharif), the place from which the Prophet Mohammad ascended to heaven.

I remember how devout Jews would line up in front of the Western Wailing Wall wearing long black suits and big black hats, or *kippahs*, to pray with the Holy Torah, bowing and sticking small pieces of paper—their messages to God—in the many small holes in the wall.

I remember, and I pray for peace in Jerusalem and Palestine, that my voice will offer *amal*—hope. I pray that my story will open doors. I lift my heart and hope for the City of God. The symbol of Palestine is the olive tree, the tree of eternity, the tree of life, peace, hope, and survival. It endures for centuries, and then, even when it appears dead, life returns from its roots. I pray that Palestine will be reborn from all of its deep roots.

Jerusalem and Olivet (taken between 1934 and 1939)

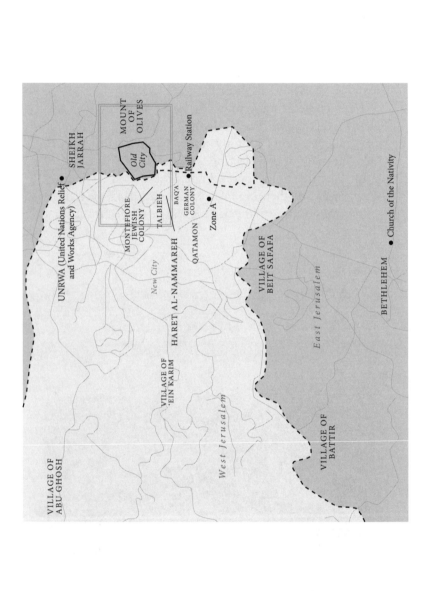

VILLAGE OF
ABU GHOSH

UNRWA (United Nations Relief
and Works Agency)

SHEIKH
JARRAH

MOUNT
OF
OLIVES

Old
City

MONTEFIORE
JEWISH
COLONY

TALBIEH

BAQA

Railway Station

German Colony

QATAMON

Zone A

HARET AL-NAMMAREH

New City

VILLAGE OF
'EIN KARIM

West Jerusalem

VILLAGE OF
BATTIR

VILLAGE OF
BEIT SAFAFA

East Jerusalem

BETHLEHEM

Church of the Nativity

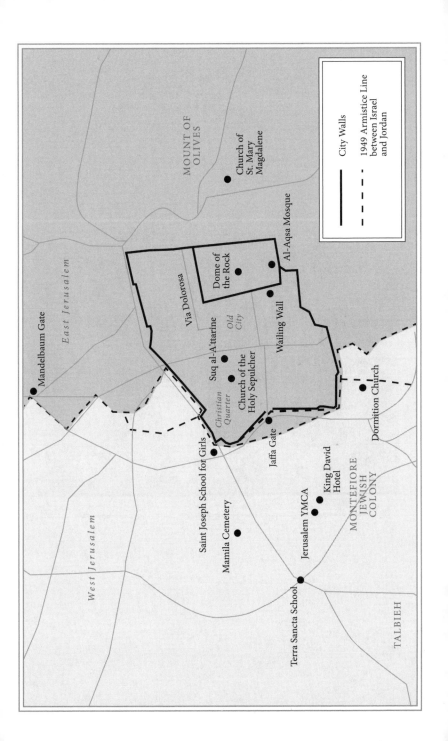

PALESTINIAN LOSS OF LAND 1946 TO 2005

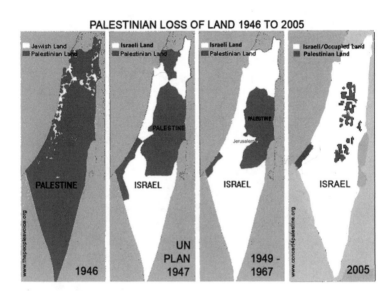

NOTES

† From my personal interviews, conversations, and correspondence with family and friends.

¹ Jacob Nammar, "Remembering Haret al-Nammareh," *Jerusalem Quarterly* 41 (Spring 2010).

² Mazin B. Qumsiyeh, *Sharing the Land of Canaan: Human Rights and the Israeli-Palestinian Struggle* (London: Pluto Press, 2004), 8.

³ Rochelle Davis, "Memories of Communal Relations in Jerusalem Prior to 1948," *Jerusalem Quarterly* 10 (Fall 2000): 21.

⁴ Anthony R. Ferris, ed., *Kahlil Gibran: A Self-Portrait* (New York: The Citadel Press, 1969), 3.

⁵ Avi Shlaim, *Israel and Palestine* (New York: Verso Books, 2009), 58

⁶ Ilan Pappe, *The Ethnic Cleansing of Palestine* (Oxford: Oneworld Publications, 2006), 23

⁷ Pappe, *The Ethnic Cleansing of Palestine*, 90–91.

⁸ Benny Morris, *The Birth of the Palestinian Refugee Problem, 1947–1949* (Cambridge: Cambridge University Press, 1988), 230.

⁹ Karen Armstrong, *Jerusalem: One City, Three Faiths* (New York: Ballantine Books, 1997).

¹⁰ Benny Morris, *1948: A History of the First Arab-Israel War* (New York: Yale University Press, 2008), 163.

[11] Arwa Aburawa, "The Great Book Robbery of 1948," *Electronic Intifada,* November 9, 2010. http://electronicintifada.net/

[12] Rochelle Davis, "The Growth of the Western Communities, 1917–1948," in *Jerusalem 1948: The Arab Neighborhoods and their Fate in the War* (Institute of Jerusalem Studies and BADIL Resource Center, 2002).

[13] Count Bernadotte, United Nation mediator, was assassinated by a Jewish terrorist gang under the leadership of Yitzhak Shamir, the man who later became prime minister of Israel. He paid for his life because he reported that, "It would be an offence against the principles of elemental justice if these innocent [Palestinian] victims of the conflict were denied the right to return to their homes, while Jewish immigrants flow into Palestine." A few weeks after his death the United Nations General Assembly passed Resolution 194 demanding the return of the Palestinian refugees to their homes and the compensation for their losses. In addition, the resolution to grant Israel admission as a member to the United Nations was contingent on its adherence to
Resolution 194, which it has disregarded ever since.

[14] All Jewish men and women must serve in the military at the age of eighteen.

[15] Unfortunately, Israel had since desecrated and destroyed the cemetery by building an "Independence Park" and subsequently an urban road through it, major electrical cables over the graves, and a parking lot over yet another part. Recently, another fifteen hundred graves have been cleared in several nighttime operations to make way for a $100 million future "Museum of Tolerance and Human Dignity" over the graves.

[16] Erskine Childers, "The Other Exodus," *Spectator* (May 12, 1961).

[17] Ferris, *Khalil Gibran,* 26.

[18] Nadine Saliba, "From Tunisia: An Ode to Revolution and Love," *La Voz de Esperanza* (March 2011). Nadine reminded me of al-Shabi's poem, "The Will of Life." This version is translated by Elliott Colla.